CONNECT!

How to Quickly Collaborate
For Success in Business and Life

Barry J. Moline

outskirts
press

CONTENTS

PART 1.
AND IN CONCLUSION...

*The Executive Summary, with exercises
to quickly get individuals and teams
on track for effective collaboration*

L et's just cut to the chase. Here's the secret to powerful connection, and getting along with others in business and life:

1. Share Personal Stories: Get closer to and learn about others, where they're from, some life experiences and interests, and also share the same about yourself.

2. Talk Equally: Be conscious of the amount of time everyone speaks, and guide interactions so individuals share about the same amount of time. Officially, it's called "Equity of Voice." The amount of time each person speaks doesn't have to be precise or forced, and it works best when it occurs naturally or is steered lightly.

3. <u>Assume Positive Intent</u>: People generally want their colleagues and peers to succeed, and are not out to get you. Since you can control only your behavior, interact with the expectation that everyone is positive and striving for a win-win outcome.

4. <u>Persist</u>: It takes time, and it works. For many, it works right away. For others, it may take longer. Keep trying. It may not work overnight, but in almost all cases, it does work eventually.

Share Personal Stories

Most of us need to work together with people to get something done. When we have a task before us, generally, we like to do it as quickly and efficiently as possible, working well with others, and accomplishing the goals of our organizations. Basically, we need to connect with people to get something done.

Let's say you're at work and you and four colleagues are assigned to conduct research and write a report. Or perhaps you five are assigned to organize a major conference for hundreds of industry peers. Maybe the group has to develop a sales plan, or a communications plan, and everyone has their own ideas about how to create it. In each case, the opportunity for conflict and friction can occur at any moment on any task.

Consider the opposite of connection. It's the silo, or what I call "silo-ization." It could be the silo of hoarding information, the silo of not sharing, the silo of independence, the silo of I-win-you-lose, the silo of wanting to be the one who gets all, or at least most, of the credit. How do you avoid the tendency toward the silo and instead create a high functioning team?

Easy. Personal stories

Sit down with your colleagues, one-on-one or in a group, and ask a few questions:

- How did you get here, working at this job?
- Where did you grow up?
- Where did you go to school?
- Tell me about yourself.
- How was your weekend?
- What's up for the coming weekend?
- If you're at a social gathering, and you're not sure if someone works outside the home or might be retired, ask "What interesting things have your attention these days?"
- If you're in a religious setting, you could ask "What was your first (church/synagogue/house of worship), and how did you come to this congregation?"
- Then share the same information about yourself. It's possible you will find interests in common, and even if you don't you will reach a deeper understanding of each other.

In her book *Captivate*, Vanessa Van Edwards presents additional techniques for engaging with people, focusing on first impressions.[1] Rather than asking people where they are

---

[1] *Captivate, The Science of Succeeding with People*, Vanessa Van Edwards, Portfolio/ Penguin Books, 2017

from or what brings them here, she suggests conversation "sparkers," such as:

- What was the highlight of your day today?
- What passionate projects are you working on?
- What exciting thing is coming up in your life?
- Do you have any vacations coming up? Or, where did you go on your last vacation?
- What got your attention this past week?
- What do you like to do to unwind?

The purpose of these questions is to get people excited and engaged, and to do so in a creative way that allows the conversation to move more deeply, and quicker.

There's another technique Edwards suggests that can work to draw people into the conversation. She calls them "Hot Buttons," which are personal topics of interest, a technique common in the world of sales.[2] The method requires you to listen carefully and comment on what your conversation partner recently said, with the intent to investigate further and get to know them better. In a sales environment, you want to find out what the immediate problem is, so you can help solve it. On the other hand, in a social gathering you want to understand what your partner likes and wants. In conversation, both are relevant—that is, the conversation can be serious, because someone might divulge an illness or family situation. Or, it can be stimulating, as they talk excitedly about a favorite hobby, interesting project,

---

[2] *5 Business Hot Buttons That Lead Straight to The Sale,* Roland Eva, March 5, 2018, blog.startuppulse.net

fun travels, or current events and the news. Here are a few examples that require listening, reflecting, and digging deeper:

- You mentioned that you volunteer at the animal shelter. How long have you done that? How did you get involved? Do you have any pets? Tell me about them.
- I heard you ask the bartender about New Zealand wines. Do you know a lot about wines? What are your favorites?
- You have a very interesting name. Is it a family name? Where are you from?

A word on listening. It's touted as the big thing, the action we need to take to be engaged in conversation. As a person who—I admit about myself—is not always a great listener, I have found a different strategy with the same outcome. *Be curious.* When you are curious about something or someone, you want to know more, and when you investigate further, guess what? You listen. So if listening is not your thing, adopt a different attitude, one of curiosity.

Flipping the perspective—when you are introducing yourself to someone—and you want a conversation starter, include an interesting tidbit about you.[3]

- If it's work, say your name and organization (and maybe your title), which are fairly standard, and then say how your work has an impact in some way.

---

[3] Idea inspired by: *How to Introduce Yourself So You'll be Unforgettable (in A Good Way!)*, Kara Cutruzzula, ideas.ted.com, July 26, 2018

Nearly everything works and will likely inspire a question or conversation.

- If you're in human resources or management, you can say "I'm Ginger Root, ACME's HR Director, and I solve people problems."
- If you're a junior analyst, or in the financial side of the organization, you can say "I'm Derek Digger with Best and Better, and I crunch the numbers."
- If you're the boss, you can say "I'm Barney Sniggles, head of Frump and Frump, and I keep all the balls in the air."
- If you work anywhere in health care, you can say "…and I help heal people."
- If you're in the energy business, you can say "and I help keep the lights on."

- If it's a social gathering, say your name and then something interesting about yourself.
  - "I'm Sarah Simil, Master Quilter."
  - "I'm Raphael Ortega, Kayaking Enthusiast."
  - "I'm Jamil Johnson, Professional People Watcher."
  - You could also choose a hobby or sport, like reading, woodworking, running, dog walking, photography, or swimming.

You're probably thinking, *It can't be that easy.*

It is. Just give it a little advanced thought.

When it comes to sharing stories, let's recognize it's not always convenient to sit down with a coworker and have a deep conversation about each other's background. It might feel weird. Often we are so busy that we don't take the time to show we care about our colleagues or find out even the slightest bits of information about what's going on in their lives. Nevertheless, when you do it, however small, you begin to connect, and it's based on caring. When you have a caring connection with a colleague, you also want to help each other succeed. It's natural. You begin to know their heart, where they are "coming from," and recognize they are not evil or have some ulterior motive to be better than you. Furthermore, they learn to like and accept you, and as a result, you both choose to perform better and support each other.

And when the situation is flipped and you're introducing yourself, have some fun. Be the catalyst that starts the conversation by sharing a personal interest of yours.

Equity of Voice: Talk the Same Amount of Time

Have you ever been in a group dominated by a single person? Individuals try to get a word in edgewise but are interrupted or dominated by the talkative one. Teammates glare at each other. Eye rolls ensue. It's a drag on productivity and there is limited progress toward accomplishing the group's goal.

The philosophy of "Equity of Voice" is that when individuals are trying to get something done in a group, or team, there's a much greater chance of success if every participant talks about the same amount of time.[4] For example, in a group of five, everyone should seek to speak one-fifth of the time and listen four-fifths of the time.[5]

While a worthy goal, this isn't always possible. Frequently, when groups convene the topic shifts, with one or two people being the subject matter experts on a particular issue. Thus, the specialists may naturally talk more. In fact, members of the group might *want* them to talk more so that everyone can learn as much and as quickly as possible from the experts. However, when everyone on the team has similar information, or gets up to speed on the topic, the group should seek equity of voice. This will improve the group's success.

There are several ways to achieve equity of voice. First, tell people about it, and that it's important for everyone to be aware of the time they are talking and listening. Reminding a group about equity of voice—the goal of sharing equally— will get people in the right state of mind. "Equity of Voice" could also be written at the top of a white board or on a piece of paper posted in the room as a visual reminder.

A second step would be to designate a "facilitator" or "guide" who lightly directs the conversation. In something like a staff meeting, this should not result in strong facilitation, where you don't want people raising their hands and being called on to speak. Rather, someone simply needs to take responsibility to be aware of the give and take. If an individual is speaking too much, for example, the guide

---

[4] *Equity of Voice in Collaboration,* Scott Hutcheson, PhD, April 4, 2017, scotthutcheson. squarespace.com
[5] *Equity of Voice and Why It Matters,* Kate Frykberg, January 9, 2017, kate.frykberg.co.nz

might ask others to be involved by asking a quiet staffer, "what do you think, Dani?" The guide's actions should not be too obvious or overbearing. The best teams try to share equally on their own,[6] and while this can happen organically, it's okay to lightly direct. If equity of voice feels imposed, people may feel like they need to wait their turn and it can limit exchange of ideas; if they're encouraged to speak, or to let others speak, it moves group discussion in a more natural direction.

I once worked in an office where the team was high performing, and on many issues, everyone wanted to participate. It was an opinionated group, and also respectful. In an amusing moment during an engaging meeting, we decided to use the concept of the Native American Talking Stick, where the person with the stick has the floor to speak, uninterrupted, and others must wait their turn.[7] In our case we didn't actually have a stick, but instead, used a small bottle of mustard someone picked up from a luncheon they attended, and it was on the conference room table because sometimes we held lunch meetings there. When a member of our team felt they needed to speak their mind, they held the mustard and everyone else waited their turn to grasp the mustard and talk.

In a structured gathering like a board of directors meeting, equity of voice would be firmly controlled by the chair. The best leaders of structured meetings seek balance in contributions from all participants.

There are two potential glitches to look out for in seeking

---

[6] *A Study of Thousands of Dropbox Projects Reveals How Successful Teams Collaborate*, Adam Pah, Brian Uzzi, and Rebecca Hinds, Harvard Business Review, HBR.org, July 26, 2018
[7] Wikipedia: *Talking Stick*

equity of voice. One is where a subordinate employee may feel it is inappropriate to challenge a supervisor in front of others. For example, if Leo isn't speaking at a meeting, it may be because he disagrees with his boss, but prefers not to raise his concerns in front of others, perhaps irritating his manager. It could also be cultural, whereby some people believe they are at a certain station in the organization (or in society) and their contribution is less valued. It's important for a guide to be aware of these nuances when seeking everyone's involvement in the discussion. The guide may not want to push certain people too strongly for a contribution if they notice reluctance, are aware of sensitive relationships, or cultural concerns.

The second glitch is that some people are uncomfortable speaking in groups. I had an employee once—an expert in information technology (IT)—who refused to provide his opinion about computer issues when we discussed multi-faceted projects in the office. Victor was shy, and while I highly valued his work and opinion, he lacked confidence speaking in groups, even with people he knew well. I decided some coaching was needed. Privately, we discussed his concerns, and I made it clear that no one else in our group had any expertise in IT at his knowledge level, and therefore we greatly needed his input. That was enough to get him to speak up, although cautiously at first. Whenever we knew we were going to have an IT issue on the agenda at one of our group meetings, I reminded Victor in advance that we would need his opinion, and he should prepare to participate. With those regular reminders he obliged, and over time, came out of his shell to gain the confidence to speak up on his own.

Assume Positive Intent

Many years ago, I had an experience that changed my attitude toward people forever. My wife was out of town on a business trip, and the first morning she was traveling I went through the normal routines. Showered, shaved, turned on the news, read the newspaper, ate breakfast, brushed my teeth, got in my car, and headed off to work. I rolled up to the exit of my apartment complex and waited for an opening in the slow-moving traffic. When I thought the cars had paused enough for me, I eased on the gas, turned right, and tried to merge into traffic. Another driver had a different idea; he wasn't going to let me in, and I had to turn hard toward the curb to avoid a collision. I locked eyes with that nasty monster of a driver and yelled at him "#%&@$!" As I sat there in traffic, inching my way toward the next stoplight, I pondered what had just happened. Rather than focus on the guy who cut me off, I realized that the first word out of my mouth that morning, after being up for more than two whole hours, was an ugly cuss word. I winced. Not a good beginning to the day. Driving along, I recognized I could not control his driving or his response to traffic, but I could control mine. I decided right then I would change my behavior. I would let go of the idea that other drivers were out to get me. I figured they are in their own worlds—like I was—and are trying to do the same thing I am: get to work on time. Who knows, they might even have an emergency and need me to get out of the way. From then on, I've been a much calmer driver and a happier person and it has permeated into many parts of my life. My blood pressure is probably lower as a result.

All this is to say if we assume other people are not out to get us, the world becomes an easier place to live. The name for this assertive behavior is "Assume Positive Intent," where we believe other people mean well and they are making decisions with their best intentions.[8, 9, 10]

Unfortunately, we've been conditioned to be suspicious that others have some agenda of which they are trying to convince others. This can make us feel threatened and put us on the defensive. Such a feeling is usually associated with a lack of information or historical expectations, and in order to combat it, we need to learn more in those situations.

Assuming positive intent is vital for connecting. When you learn more about why a person wants to take a particular action, you can seek more information, learn the reasons for the direction they are taking, and better understand what they are trying to accomplish. You feel more open and connected. By asking more questions and seeking understanding, you build trust.

When you're faced with a situation where you are unaware what the intent of another person might be, do the following:

1. Assume positive intent. Take a deep breath and believe they are interested in decisions and actions that create a win-win outcome and are seeking to improve whatever situation is facing them.

---

[8] *3 Benefits In My Life From Assuming Positive Intent,* Tom Blair Blog, February 15, 2018
[9] *The Hidden Power of Assuming Positive Intent,* Bruce Eckfeldt, Forbes Magazine, August 15, 2017
[10] *The Power of Assuming Positive Intent,* Claire Lew, Know Your Company Blog, November 30, 2017

2. Approach them with respect and ask if you can talk with them about the situation.
3. Ask questions. What's your goal? What are you try-ing to accomplish here? What information leads you toward that decision?
4. Listen carefully. Try to understand the person's per-spective and why they are choosing this particular outcome. Learn as much as you can. Say "Tell me more."
5. Provide other relevant information if you have it. And when the opportunity arises, discuss additional options. When presenting new ideas, say "Consider this."

It can be more work and take more intellectual effort to overcome the friction that comes from assuming positive in-tent, but it's worth it. You are creating positive energy in the relationship which, ultimately, strengthens the actions you take. You also become a better leader, co-worker, family member, and person.

Building Team Members' Interest in Each Other

Here's one activity you can do to help a group stay in touch with what's going on in each other's lives. At the be-ginning of a meeting, give everyone one to two minutes to share something going on that is somewhat personal. The amount of time is important; keep it short. The facilitator or guide, usually the supervisor (but it doesn't have to be), loosely keeps track of the time so no one dominates and everyone shares somewhat equally. A few possible topics: travel, recent or upcoming weekend activities, kids, pets, and hobbies. Keep it light. The value is that people who already know each other continue to learn about and stay interested in each other. Sometimes their interests might even overlap. This builds cohesiveness and creates opportunity for serendipity among teammates.

Helping a Fluctuating Team with a "Connected Roster"

Sometimes we work with a group of people—perhaps creating a task force that meets monthly—that fluctuates attendance based on changing interest. Over time, the group might expand or people may depart. If people don't know each other, or if there are a lot of people attending, it may be too tedious and time consuming for the individuals at each meeting to share what's going on in their lives. Another option to help people connect is to create a "Connected Roster," where everyone provides their basic information—name, organization, phone, email—and also briefly describes their professional interests, and most important, some personal interests. The Connected Roster is a tool—a contact list—that also serves as a continuous ice breaker to help individuals on the task force quickly learn a few interests of their colleagues. When people see a glimpse of each other's lives, connected conversations can more easily develop at meeting breaks, providing the opportunity for individuals to find something in common, or at least to be curious about members of the group.

Connected Roster

Name	Organization	Phone	Email	Interests
Barry Moline	Connect!	800-555-1234	ConnectBarryMoline @gmail.com	Professional: Reduce the impacts of climate change Personal: Hockey, hiking, guitar, travel, Spanish, pickleball, reading

Using "Fun Facts" to Quickly Get a New Group Talking

Fun Facts is an activity a new group can use to quickly break the ice and get people talking to each other, and more easily work together. Before a new group convenes, a leader emails everyone and asks them to provide one to two interesting things about themselves from their life, either recent or an earlier time. For example, playing tennis with a famous person, appearing on a TV show, having a mix up with a birth certificate, an unusual hobby like flower arranging, playing a sport, visiting an unusual place like Antarctica, or serving in the Peace Corps. Then during the first meeting of the group and at breaks, the leader reads a few of the fun facts and everyone has the chance to guess who it is. Subsequently, when the group interacts socially, the fun facts help to initiate conversation. Colleagues become curious and want to know more, breaking the ice for other collaboration to take place.

While the activity is useful in professional settings, it is particularly effective with groups where employment status is uncertain. That is, a mix of people who are students, working, retired, or unemployed.

Toby Ayash, international tour group leader, uses fun facts to get groups of 20-30 strangers to quickly get to know each other. "When people learn something interesting about each other, starting a conversation becomes so easy, it's almost irresistible," said Ayash. "It really brings people together, and you see bonds created that would never have formed on their own."[11]

Improve Your Relationships—Say "Hey"

This is a good exercise to expand your personal relationships as well as grow your emotional intelligence (i.e., quickly picking up on the feelings of others). If you're a supervisor, they sometimes call this activity "management by walking around." If you're a peer, it's just getting to know your fellow work mates.

Take responsibility to stop by your colleagues' offices or workspaces and just say "hey, Amara," or "good morning, Fernando." Doing this at the beginning of the day is widely accepted. A natural second question is to ask about their weekend (past or upcoming), or perhaps an activity you were aware of, like a concert they attended. You don't have to go much further in the conversation. Again, keep it light, and you'll develop a slightly deeper understanding of your colleagues. Then when it comes time to work together, the conversation will start from a more positive relationship platform.

---

[11] Interview with Toby Ayash, April 11, 2019

In a study of 1,000 workers, 39% felt a greater sense of belonging when their colleagues regularly checked in with them.[12] Stopping by someone's office or desk to see how coworkers are doing is the most effective tactic for improving the sense of inclusion. It doesn't matter their age or gender. We can connect better with fellow employees and make them feel valued by reaching out on a personal level, just by saying "hey."

Onboarding New Employees

<u>Personal Stories</u>: The next time a new employee joins your team, gather in a staff meeting and take turns in a round-table discussion. Set a timer for two minutes and have everyone share a story about their background. You can even do this a few times around if you like. What's important is that no one dominates and that everyone participates. Employees with a long tenure in the organization can still find new and interesting experiences to share. Even if their stories have already been told, they will be new to the teammate you are onboarding, and will remind others of their colleagues' interesting backgrounds. This kind of story sharing is the beginning of breaking the ice that is needed for everyone in the office to learn a little more about each other and aspire to work as a team.

<u>Personal Journey</u>. Another activity to achieve cohesiveness as a group is for everyone to describe one or more events in their lives that have had a profound impact on

---

[12] *The Surprising Power of Simply Asking Coworkers How They're Doing,* Karyn Twaronite, EY Global Diversity & Inclusiveness Officer, Harvard Business Review, HBR.org, February 28, 2019

establishing their values and who they are personally. This leads to describing each person's foundation, which often overlap. Keep the journeys to a modest length, where everyone shares about the same amount of time. In a variation, you can put a timeline showing decades at the top of a whiteboard, give each person a different color pad of Post-it Notes, have them note their high-impact events and post them on the timeline. Then everyone takes turn talking about their journey, noting the highlights.

Enjoy Networking

There are a lot of techniques for networking, but one I find particularly interesting is presented by leadership blogger and speaker Jeremiah Miller.[13] In his Forging Leaders blog, he describes how much he used to hate networking, or at least business events where vendors and prospects are expected to meet a lot of people in a short amount of time, engaging in small, superficial queries, such as "What do you do?" and "What business are you in?" Miller describes how much he dislikes those events, even calling them torture. For many people who are introverts, networking can be tough.

Miller changed his approach to where he now flips the process around. Rather than trying to meet a lot of people at networking events, he seeks to meet only a few, but have longer and deeper conversations. He doesn't even try to pass out his business card but waits until someone requests it. And instead of asking "What do you do?" he asks:

---

[13] *How to Network if You Hate Networking,* Jeremiah Miller, Forging Leaders Blog, April 17, 2016

- What do you love about your job?
- If you were giving a speech, what would you talk about?
- Have you ever met a famous person? Tell me about it.
- What was your first job, when you were a kid?
- If you could be anywhere in the world, where would that be and what would you be doing?

As he seeks to learn a few deeper thoughts and experiences about others, he finds they frequently ask questions about him as well.

Miller is curious about people. He talks less and listens more. And he now feels differently about networking events:

- He believes he has more confidence, because instead of selling himself, he's just interested in other people.
- He's built deeper relationships, and aside from learning about other people, they also want to know more about him.
- He now enjoys networking, because he feels he's going to meet an interesting person.

Miller's twist on networking uses the technique of sharing personal stories to engage with others more deeply.

Remember Names

Do you know what your favorite word is? Your name. But why are many people bad at remembering names? It's so important in networking and group dynamics, yet many of us are bad at it. If you want to improve your conversations, learn people's names; it will make a difference in the quickness and ease with which you engage. Here are five ways to improve:[14]

- Meet and repeat. Use their name as soon as possible in the conversation. "Nice to meet you, Jason!"
- Spell the name in your head. If someone has an unusual name, ask how to spell it. Getting someone's name correct is a high compliment, particularly for unusual names, so take the time to think about how to spell and say it.
- Imagine a visual bumper sticker: Cheryl from Santa Fe, Bill from Jasper, Joan with the red hair.
- Connect them to someone you already know: Associate their name with another person you know or have heard of. Bill (like Billy Joel), or Emily (like my daughter). You can also put it together with an image, like Lily (and think of the flower).
- Care about remembering names. If you believe learning names is important, you'll make the effort. Try a few techniques, and you'll definitely get better.

Train Yourself

You might be thinking… this other person is so hard to reach, this effort is too difficult. And you may be right, some people are difficult. Mostly, that's because no one has ever really tried to get to know them. This is your place of

---

[14] *The Five Best Tricks to Remember Names*, Kristi Hedges, Forbes, August 21, 2013, Forbes.com

employment, or perhaps a community or religious group. You don't have to be best friends or even friends at all. The goal is to seek a basic level of understanding, and that's it. Nothing more. This is do-able.

If you have ever tried to train a dog, you quickly learn the most important ingredient: training yourself. They say, there are no bad dogs, only bad owners. If you want to teach a dog to listen to you, try this. Let's assume your dog knows how to sit. Put food in their bowl, tell them to sit, then count to ten. At ten, point to the bowl and say, "Eat!"

Step one, of course, is getting over the look of your sweet puppy when it's seemingly dying of hunger and you are cruelly counting to ten while delaying them from eating. You are training *yourself* to not worry about your dog's cute face, which may cause you to give in and let him eat. You are also training your dog to listen to you. It works. You both learn that you—the human—is in charge, and when you want to train your dog to do other things, like not jumping on strangers, you can use a similar technique.

But there *is* a problem. Learning to count to ten, especially doing it at *every* meal, is difficult. Nevertheless, if you can train yourself and stay consistent, you can also learn to ask questions about your colleagues and share personal stories. You can be that facilitator or guide, aware of the time people spend sharing, helping everyone to achieve equity of voice in the amount of time they spend talking. Train yourself to use and share personal stories all the time, and you'll develop the habit. Then when you need your team to work on a new project, they will care enough about each other to do a good job—for each other.

Persist

Despite your best efforts at reaching out, it takes some people extra time to warm up to others. That's their problem, not yours. Be patient and keep trying. They will come around. It's tough, and like training that dog by counting to ten, after you repeatedly try to break the ice and show you care about them—just a bit, just enough—eventually they will come around.

It sounds so easy. "They will come around." *LOL*, you're probably thinking, *you have not met Julia! And Larry! He's a tough one!* I'm telling you, it doesn't matter. It works in most situations. It might take a few weeks or months, but it will work eventually. You just cannot give up. Persist.

———————— **"** ————————

For some people you interact with, if they think you're weak, they are going to walk all over you. There are times when you have to stand up to a bully.[15]

Joy Ditto, CEO, Arlington, Virginia

Occasionally It Doesn't Work Quickly Enough—Or Maybe Not at All

Let's admit that there are cases and situations, there are certain people, who are just plain difficult. They want nothing to do with personal stories about their life or anyone else's, and they just want to either move forward to get the job done or do it themselves, alone. There are still ways to

---

[15] Interview with Joy Ditto, CEO, Arlington, Virginia, October 2015

connect with them in a professional way. But it will take time, and sometimes more time than you, your business, or community group has to give. In those situations, you need to be able to evaluate the circumstances and be ready to change course, change personnel, or change the goals of the project.

We must face reality and not kid ourselves. While writing this book, I interviewed nearly 100 people from all over the United States. Most were eager to discuss their personal style, their philosophy, and their experience connecting and collaborating with others. A few told me it doesn't work all the time. There are some people out there, they said, who are just too challenging to work with. "They are pills," one person told me. "I leave them alone, and I'm happier."

At first I disagreed. No one, I thought, was beyond working with, beyond trying to get to know. However, I've come to realize that there are some people who just take a really really long time to warm up to. Ultimately, they lack trust, and they've had experiences that have led them to distance themselves and avoid working with others. These are the people you should give time to and perhaps even stay a safe distance from. Treat them with respect, bring them closer when possible, give them an occasional compliment when it's deserved, and try to build trust.

Trust is best explained by the expression "Do what you say and say what you do." That is, if you are consistently straightforward, open to ideas, stick to your agreements and are ethical, then over time others will recognize you are someone they can work with. For people who don't easily trust, this can take a long time. You may have to work around them for a while, but nevertheless, seek to always include them.

Your actions are solely within your control, and you should take responsibility for them. Here are a few other options:[16]

- Do your job well. It's a way to build respect among your peers. If you are not performing in your job, others may think less of you, so first you must be a contributing member of your team.
- Offer to help co-workers with a project, but make it clear, only if they want it. You should not be offering help because *you* think *they* need it. Just offer assistance to help make the work better or faster, and most of all, be sincere.
- Compliment your problem person. When they have a good idea, refer to it; perhaps something like this: "As Bill just said, I think we need to call our customers and learn how they're dealing with this issue." Confirm Bill's idea and the relationship ice may begin to thaw.
- Think the best of the other person. Sometimes we imagine others are out to get us. In reality, most people don't give us much thought. They're busy thinking about themselves. When you begin to filter the actions of others in a positive way, or at least in a neutral manner, then your attitude changes. You may see that they actually try to help, but it's just not coming out in the way you think it should. Give them the benefit of the doubt. Assume positive intent.
- Kill them with kindness. When you genuinely show compassion, it is effective on two levels. First, being

---

[16] *What to do When a Workplace Relationship Breaks Down,* Scott Maxwell, ABC Life, abc.net.au

nice assures you are making the effort. Second, it's a consistent strategy where you always present a positive, pleasant demeanor. Everyone can see you are sincere.

- If someone lies or is deceptive, calmly return the focus of conversation back to the truth. Ask them questions about their sources to better understand where they are getting their information. In the conversation, provide evidence that is factual, and avoid mixing in opinions. Say, "That's not my understanding of the situation. Let's share what we know so we can distinguish the facts and determine what information is missing." The goal is to turn the deceiver into a joint problem-solver. The only way to confront someone stating myths and fabrications is to calmly yet relentlessly return the conversation back to facts and reality.

- If all else fails, get help. Go to your manager, or depending on the chain of command, their supervisor. Go to human resources, particularly if it gets personal, which is unacceptable in the workplace. If you do so, focus on facts. If nothing works, and you two must remain working together, perhaps structured training or even counseling can help. Many organizations offer communications and human dynamics training. Strained workplace relationships reduce the company's performance, and we want our organizations to succeed. Addressing these issues is in everyone's best interest.

I've worked with a few difficult individuals over the

span of four decades in the workforce, and fortunately, I can count them on one hand. Nevertheless, it's distressing for people like you and me who want to work with others, to be rebuffed, particularly when we believe that effectively working together produces better results. What I've found most effective over the years is to be patient. Some people need time—a lot of time—to find comfort and trust with others. Sometimes the relationship starts out on the wrong foot, with a negative interaction. Perhaps the two of you sought the same promotion and you got it—and he or she resents you for it. Whatever the situation, if you don't give up and do what you can to keep the lines of communication open, in the long run you will have a greater chance of success even with the toughest relationships.

Eventually the opportunity to connect may arise. When you have built up trust, you will be the one who can bring the other person into the situation, the group, or the team, resolving a problem or building on a new idea. And remember, if you don't take the initiative—if you don't persist—it may never happen. Connecting takes persistence.

The Magic of "Consider This"

There is one technique that can help to diffuse conversations so they change from "you vs. me" to "Let's work on this interesting idea together." It's the phrase "Consider this."

Let's say you're in a conversation with a difficult person. Because they may not like or trust you, they disagree with everything you say. The reason is because they see the outcome of the conversation to be where you may win, and they don't want to be the one losing. If you're working on a project together, and you want to move the conversation forward, say "Consider this" when you want to present an idea. It's a form of brainstorming. Instead of the idea being yours, put it out there between the two of you, for both of you to examine together. It's like saying "Here's something I heard on CNN." That is, it's not my idea... It's coming from elsewhere, and let's take a look at it together. Saying "Consider this" can de-escalate the conflict between you vs. them and moves it in the direction where both of you can examine the same idea equally.

Should You Read the Rest of This Book?

In this book I present 14 eyebrow-raising, almost unreal but absolutely true case studies, about people who came from opposite environments, thought differently, yet found a way to work together, help each other, perform better together, and accomplish more. Now you know the basics. Read the rest of the book to see how others used these techniques to work more safely, improve productivity, reject hatred, and even begin to do the improbable—get Republicans and Democrats in Congress to work together.

There's another reason why you should read the rest of the book: You need to convince yourself that connecting works, and that it will benefit you.

The concept is called "self-persuasion."[17] A lot of research suggests that we don't simply believe what others tell

[17] *The Power of Self-Persuasion,* Aronson, E. (1999). American Psychologist, 54(11), 875-884

us, and particularly what anonymous strangers (like me) tell you.[18, 19] Rather, you need to take in information at a pace and schedule most comfortable to you. You need to recognize your doubts and let the case studies speak to your life experience. Then you should decide for yourself—are these ideas and stories of real-life examples sufficient for you to act and change the way you interact with others? Only after answering this question might you take the suggestions presented here to develop your own method of connecting.

The examples will show you how to seek a higher level of connection in your work, in your community, and in your life.

—————————— 66 ——————————

We sometimes think collaboration will be easy, and everyone's going to get along hunky-dory, singing Kumbaya in three-part harmony. When you apply it in real life, we find that life is messy. Collaboration takes dedication and clear vision.[20]
Erick Rheam, Motivational Speaker, Indiana

[18] *Self-Persuasion as Marketing Technique: The Role of Consumers' Involvement,* Stefan F. Bernritter, Iris van Ooijen, and Barbara C.N. Müller, (2017) European Journal of Marketing, Vol. 51 Issue: 5/6, pp. 1075-1090
[19] *Strategies to Build Intrinsic Motivation,* David Palank, Edutopia, September 2, 2015
[20] Interview with Erick Rheam, Motivational Speaker, Indiana, October 2015

PART 2.
IS THERE REALLY
A PROBLEM?

"Houston, we have a problem." Those were the words spoken by Apollo 13 commander James Lovell on April 13, 1970, when a portion of the spacecraft he was flying to the moon exploded.

Today, I'd put it this way: "America, we have a problem." It's huge. And it's blowing up our relationships and our ability to be productive.

The problem is we lack civility, we are out of the habit of working together, and it has become natural to be suspicious of each other's motives. Rather than give each other the benefit of the doubt—that our intentions are worthy and valid—many people assume others are out to get them. We are near perfect while other people are jerks.

If you think I'm not talking about you, let me ask you a question. Have you listened to yourself "talking" to drivers, cyclists, and pedestrians as you travel around town? Make no mistake. Those people are crazy, and you on the other hand, are in the top 10% of perfection.

Let's admit it, there is a problem, and unless you're a disciple of Gandhi, in some way we are probably part of it. Many people have studied the situation. Let's look at the data. It's shocking.

─────────────── **"** ───────────────

There's a sense that people out in the country can see the far left and the far right [strongly disagreeing] on social media [and on television], and they think it's okay to act out any way they want.[21]
U.S. Representative Tom Rooney (R-FL)

Incivility Is Growing in Society

In their comprehensive studies entitled *Civility in America,* researchers found we are living in a society where incivility is growing. Here are the basics from their online polls over several years:[22]

- 93% of Americans say incivility is a societal issue.
- 75% say that incivility has risen to "crisis" levels, up from 65% in 2014.
- 90% of Americans say incivility leads to intimidation, threats, violence, cyberbullying, and harassment.
- 84% have personally experienced incivility.

---

[21] *This Town Melts Down,* Mark Leibovich, The New York Times, July 11, 2017
[22] *Civility in America VII: The State of Civility,* Weber Shandwick, Powell Tate, and KRC Research, January and December 2016, webershandwick.com

- 73% say the U.S. is losing stature as a civil nation.
- 97% believe it is important for the U.S. president to be civil.
- 86% agree a president's tone and level of civility impacts the reputation of the nation.
- Respondents say the top three reasons for growing incivility are politicians, the internet/social media, and the news media.

Interestingly, Americans absolve themselves from taking responsibility for the problem. Basically, the further away from the situation, the worse we think it is.

- 94% say they always or usually act politely and respectfully.
- 78% say people who they know personally either usually or always act politely and respectfully.
- 57% say people in their community always or usually act politely and respectfully.
- 24% think the American people in general either always or usually act politely and respectfully.

And to solve incivility:

- 75% would be willing to set a good example by practicing civility.
- 58% favor elimination of fake news from the internet to improve civility.
- 49% recommend civility training in schools and colleges.

These data are stark. Not only is incivility a problem, we don't recognize our part in it. By blaming other people, we are doing something dangerous: assuming the best in us and the worst in others, particularly strangers. That assumption is a core concern we must try hard to both recognize in ourselves and to overcome. Fortunately, people we hang out with are just like us: generally nice. For those we do not know, we sometimes assume they do not have our best interests at heart. Worse yet, we sometimes assume they are out to get us. This is a cycle of suspicion we must seek to change.

Strangers are not out to get you. Rather, strangers are mostly just like you. They are nice, decent people. The reason why you might think the worst is not because you are bad, it's simply because you don't know them. Rather than assume the worst, make the assumption that strangers are good people trying to do their best and generally—and here's the funny part—are either unconcerned with you or actually interested in your success. As we discussed earlier about assuming positive intent, change your attitude toward them, and your interactions will be more constructive. The good news from the data is that it appears people are willing to try.

Rudeness is Growing in the Workplace and It's Costing Billions in Wasted Time

Rudeness and incivility are growing in the workplace. In a 1998 study, one-quarter of people surveyed reported being treated rudely at work at least once per week. Thirteen years later in 2011, 55% said the same, and in 2016, that rose to

62%, nearly two-thirds.[23] *The Harvard Business Review* reports that 98% of workers have experienced rudeness in the workplace.[24] Collaboration and productivity suffer as a result, and 78% feel a decline in commitment to their employer. That's just about everybody, everywhere. The problem has gotten worse in the workplace as two trends are converging. The first is we are seeing more minorities and people of international culture in the U.S. workforce. Second, we frequently hear random and disparaging comments by President Donald J. Trump about all sorts of minorities. What we see in the news, like it or not, can impact how we act in everyday life. We too become suspicious of others, and of the stranger.

Workplace stress also costs businesses billions of dollars each year, according to the American Psychological Association.[25] When incivility goes unaddressed, organizations experience higher turnover, more sick days taken, and lower productivity. The Harvard study data suggest it's pretty bad, as 63% report lost work time avoiding the offender, and fully 80% avoid work just worrying about the offender. Even worse for the bottom line, it can lead to claims of workplace harassment, expensive legal disputes, and financial settlements. Such negativity, a University of Michigan[26] study reports, leads to higher instances of mental fatigue, defensiveness, less productivity, and a negative impact on

---

[23] *Mastering Civility: A Manifesto for the Workplace,* Christine Porath, Associate Professor, Georgetown University McDonough School of Business, Grand Central Publishing, 2017

[24] *The Price of Incivility,* Christine Porath and Christine Pearson, Harvard Business Review, January-February, 2013

[25] *The Age of Rage,* Dori Meinert, HR Magazine, April 2017, pp 27-32

[26] *Workplace Negativity Can Hurt Productivity, Russell Johnson and Andy Henion,* February 25, 2015, msutoday.msu.edu

company culture. Such negativity also has caused 25% of workers to take out frustrations on customers.

Here's an oddball example that shows the financial impact of rudeness and poor collaboration. DeMarcus Cousins is an All-Star player in the National Basketball Association. In his career with the Sacramento Kings and New Orleans Pelicans, he developed a reputation as a disruptor in the locker room, fighting with teammates and staff. It's reported he is difficult to coach, but he's been given a pass on much of this bad behavior because he is very talented.[27] On July 1, 2018, Cousins became a free agent. A marquee player worth $25-30 million per year, he received no offers. Teams said he wasn't "right for their culture," which really translates to "he is bad for team chemistry." Or to put it bluntly, he doesn't get along well with others. Cousins ended up signing with the Golden State Warriors for $5.3 million, 80% below his value just a few months earlier. That's a loss of $20 million per year, basically because of rudeness. If you're thinking what I'm thinking… For $20 million per year, I can be very nice. Heck, for just $1 million I think most people would be an angel.

Kids Are Getting Worse at Relating Face-to-Face

We live in a growing technological world where the vast majority of Americans (and First-World citizens) have smart phones. We text, Snapchat, Tweet, Facebook, Facetime, YouTube, WhatsApp, Google, and basically interact with

---

[27] *The Real Cost of Bad Behavior: DeMarcus Cousins Loses Out On $20 Million,* Don Yaeger, Contributor, Forbes Magazine, July 6, 2018, forbes.com

our phones as a communications method in a way that was not imagined just a decade ago. Screens are so ubiquitous that it has impacted not only the *way* we communicate, but it has altered and even reduced *our ability* to communicate.

Research is beginning to show the impact, and in a nutshell, it's bad. Findings everywhere show that technology is having a negative impact on the quality and quantity of face-to-face communication.

In a survey of 100 students at Elon University, research reported the following:[28]

- 92% believe technology negatively affects face-to-face communication.
- 89% believe there is a degradation in the quality of conversation in the presence of technology.
- 73% of students eating dinner with friends spent time texting or using their computers or tablet.

Other observations include:

- Students use technology as a crutch to hide behind.
- Many believe, nevertheless, it is disrespectful to use technology in the presence of others—even though they do it.
- Some have tried to occasionally disengage during meals, creating a "cell-phone tower," where everyone stacks their phones together while they dine, focusing the conversation on each other.

---

[28] *The Effect of Technology on Face-to-Face Communication,* Emily Drago, The Elon Journal, Elon University, Spring 2015

Why is this a problem? One concern is that a large percentage of communication—some say more than 90%—is
visual or tonal. That is, we get a lot of context from both
tone of voice and facial expressions. Words alone are just
a fraction of the constellation of communication we need
to engage and understand with a conversation partner. That
explains why it's possible to watch a soap opera in another language, for example, and differentiate a happy vs. sad
scene, and within reason, generally have a feel for what is
happening in the show, just by watching facial expressions
and listening for tone of voice. In other words, to communicate effectively we need to talk to each other, not just email,
text, or tweet.

Implications will be felt in the future, as students enter
the workforce less able to communicate with fellow employees and colleagues. We may easily find young adults with
limited social skills, who are awkward in a person-to-person
interaction.

France's leaders recognized this growing problem and
took action. In August 2018, French lawmakers outlawed
smartphones in all schools for students between the ages
of three to fifteen. Reflecting on the new law, Jean-Michel
Blanquer, France's education minister, said he wanted children to rediscover connections to nature, to doing things with
their hands, and to have contact with other human beings.[29]
A study by the London School of Economics and Political
Science found that banning smartphones in schools resulted

---

[29] *Should Kids Be Allowed to Have Smartphones in School? France is Banning Them from the Classroom,* Char Adams, August 15, 2018

in clear improvement in students' test scores.[30] France is expecting such improvement.

The bottom line is that the young, and Millennials entering the workforce, are losing the ability to carry on face-to-face conversations with other human beings. This impacts their ability to think and communicate in real time, with fewer skills in conversing and discussing issues. The ability to pick up on non-verbal cues is also diminishing, and perhaps, even the ability to focus attention on another person. The concern is not specific to the young, as adults increasingly spend more time online than speaking to each other. It appears to be a growing epidemic that we need to continue to understand, stay aware of as it happens, and be methodical about confronting and changing. Sharing personal stories is one way to individually engage, and we also need to be present with others and converse with them to achieve the complete impact of social fulfillment and establish true relationships.

Rudeness Is Growing Online— Like You Didn't Know

Negative comments in the newspaper are growing as well. *The Guardian* newspaper in London studied the nature of online comments to all their articles published over a seventeen-year period, between January 1999 and March 2016.[31] The analysis was extensive, reviewing 70 million

---

[30] *Ill Communication: Technology, Distraction & Student Performance,* Louis-Philippe Beland and Richard Murphy, CEP Discussion Paper No. 1350, London School of Economics Center for Economic Performance, May 2015

[31] *The Dark Side of Guardian Comments,* The Guardian, April 12 and April 17, 2016

comments. They used an automated system searching for key words in the comments section of their news and opinion stories. What they found was that people were just plain nasty all around, to the article writer and to fellow commenters. The anonymous nature of the comment section contributes to this phenomenon. If we don't know someone, we find it easier to engage negatively, and even insult them.

I won't even depress you further with additional statistics and studies on bullying at school and cyber-bullying by young teens on Facebook and other social media platforms. One statistic is important, though: about 30% of kids report bullying in person at school or online.[32]

The Impact of President Trump's Behavior

It is difficult to ignore the impact on society of President Donald J. Trump's approach to interpersonal communication and ability—or inability—to connect. While many have strong opinions about President Trump either in support or opposition, we should examine his attention-grabbing tactics and name-calling as a choice, and evaluate its effectiveness at accomplishing his goals. Is personally connecting with people the best approach, or is encouraging animosity a more effective method? Perhaps what worked for Citizen Trump in private, confidential business is not as effective for President Trump in the public, political arena. Or maybe it is effective, but it's difficult to watch. Most important, are there elements of his approach we can learn from and use in our own opportunities to connect?

---

[32] American Society for the Positive Care of Children, Bullying Statistics and Information, americanspcc.org

This is not a treatise on why Donald Trump is a good or bad president. Obviously, the president's personal style is difficult to ignore. Some would characterize it as bullying, and in many cases, lying. But sometimes a president needs to bully. Presidents need to make deals—and yes, you can make deals and be nice. On the other hand, sometimes you need to be firm, to be negative perhaps, and stand up to the other side to get what you want. Since the beginning of politics, we've seen plenty of spirited, emotional behavior and name-calling all along the political spectrum. However, I'm not sure we've ever seen it this strong from the chief executive. The relentless insults by President Trump toward his adversaries, and even at times his allies, has the effect of imprinting this negative behavior on the nation. It can easily result in some people accepting the notion that it's okay to use a similar style to be effective. Donald Trump didn't invent insults and bullying as a strategy, but his position as president has the impact of promoting it as an approach for others to consider and more easily adopt.

In December 2018, the president had a combative, on-camera dispute with incoming Speaker of the House of Representatives Nancy Pelosi about, well, whatever. That's what politicians do, debate each other. Pelosi's response the next day was amusing, illustrative, and a cautionary flag for anyone seeking to engage in such heated conversations. She said, "You get into a tinkle contest with a skunk, you get tinkle all over you."[33] There's a similar old expression that adds an additional element: "Never wrestle with a pig. You both

---

[33] *Pelosi Introduces World to New Idiom: 'Tinkle Contest with A Skunk,'* Avery Anapol, The Hill, December 11, 2018

get dirty, *and the pig likes it*."[34] Such rhetorical battles rarely result in winners, and the only thing proved is that you can stand toe-to-toe with someone who has a strong personality. Plus, the pig—that is, the person you are arguing with—wants you to stoop to their level. Of course, sometimes you must stand up to a bully and maybe even relish it. But if it doesn't lead to any positive result, also consider the benefit of holding your words, saving your energy and emotions, and engaging in a more constructive manner.

Interestingly, First Lady Melania Trump leads an effort to prevent cyberbullying. The "Be Best" campaign seeks to encourage positive social, emotional, and physical habits, particularly online.[35] Of course, it's difficult not to contrast her message to the cyberbullying behavior of her husband, the president, from the focus of her message. His cyber-attacks on Twitter are relentless, rude, and unprecedented for the President of the United States to personally engage in such uncouth behavior. Nevertheless, his wife's pursuit is truly a noble goal, and one in sync with the thesis of this tome. To be crystal clear, as the most effective strategy to connect, this book suggests using the First Lady's model; that is, choosing words wisely in personal communication and speaking with respect and compassion. It's best to use courteous and considerate approaches in our dialogues, and avoid succumbing to insults and bullying.

When I first researched and wrote the words above, early in Donald Trump's presidency, our nation was in a state of

---

[34] This quote has been attributed to several famous authors such as Mark Twain and George Bernard Shaw, as well as President Abraham Lincoln, among others. quoteinvestigator.com

[35] whitehouse.gov/bebest

affairs I would describe as an aberration compared to any-thing we've seen in the last few decades. While there have always been strong disagreements along the political spectrum, observing the situation several years after Trump's election I would characterize the state of our civil discourse to be the worst we've seen in decades. Lulu Garcia-Navarro, host of NPR's Weekend Edition Sunday discussed this issue—and the impact of the 2016 presidential campaign on discourse today—in a segment on the influence of rhetoric in media and politics.

In the 2016 election "we saw the rhetoric being used to attack certain populations in the country: Muslims, African Americans, women, disabled reporters," said Carolyn Lukensmeyer, Executive Director at the National Institute for Civil Discourse. "We actually saw physical attacks following the kind of virulent rhetoric that we're now seeing going into the [2018] election."[36]

The Southern Poverty Law Center has correlated the Trump candidacy, campaign and presidency with the rise of hate groups. Their research shows between 2015-2018, the number of hate groups increased 30%, reaching a new high of 1,020 across the U.S.[37] Sadly, there are many types of hate groups; white nationalists alone in that time frame increased by 50%. In the previous four-year period, during the Obama presidency, there was a 23% *decline* in the number of hate groups.

---

[36] *Rhetoric in Media and Politics,* Weekend Edition Sunday, National Public Radio, October 28, 2018

[37] *Rage Against Change: White Supremacy Flourishes Amid Fears of Immigration and Nation's Shifting Demographics,* Heidi Beirich, Intelligence Report, Southern Poverty Law Center, Issue 166, Spring 2019, pp. 35-42

While we have had difficult periods in our nation, from the founders through the Civil War, the fight for civil rights in the 1950s and 1960s to today, the current era may be different. "Once the [2016 presidential] election was over, Americans who voted for Trump continued to demonize and hate Hillary voters, and vice-versa. And that's still going on today, two years later," continued Lukensmeyer.

It has even impacted the efficiency and output of workers. "The National Institute has actually had calls from major U.S. corporations, saying 'We have project innovation teams that have not come back to the same level of productivity since the [2016] election.' It's like a virus in our society. That is different and new," said Lukensmeyer.

Ariela Schachter, Assistant Professor of Sociology at Washington University in St. Louis, Mo., has researched how language informs social discussions and perceptions in the context of immigration. The way we discuss certain groups and the way racially charged words are processed by individuals has a real impact how many people view an entire segment of the population, such as immigrants.

"In one recent study with University of Chicago researcher Renee Flores, we found that white Americans overwhelmingly associate undocumented immigrants with criminality," said Schachter.[38] "This is factually unfounded and all the research points to the exact opposite. But when the President of the United States is constantly tweeting about the many criminals, terrorists and rapists coming from Mexico and Central America, it's not hard to guess what is driving this stereotype."

---

[38] *Who are the "Illegals?" The Social Construction of Illegality in the United States,* Renee D. Flores and Ariela Schachter, September 14, 2018, American Sociological Review

Flores and Schachter's research also showed that some people who were *not* Trump supporters also adopted these stereotypes. "We were really surprised by that finding," said Schachter. "We hypothesized that we would find something different." We live in 'echo chambers' where each side consumes very different news and media, and we thought that this separation would be reflected in the types of ideas that liberals versus conservatives held of immigrants, "and yet this criminality stereotype seems to have overwhelmed peoples' political divides and has invaded [everyone's] minds," said Schachter. In other words, with the continuous onslaught of President Trump's false statements connecting immigrants and criminality, and the relentless reporting about those statements by conservative, moderate, and liberal news media, even individuals not inclined to believe it strangely lean toward believing it. That is, the constant bombarding of these negative stereotypes, even though they are false, amplifies the messages and negatively influences the populous.

We could consider this simply a continuation of an effective political campaign, where we are seeing the result of saturation advertising.[39] That is, flooding the marketplace with messages in nearly every communications medium: television, YouTube, radio, news, social media, billboards, and even new product interviews, such as a cooking demonstration on a morning news show. This is frequently done for large-budget advertising campaigns like State Farm *(You're in Good Hands)*, Geico *(Fifteen minutes could save you 15% or more on car insurance)*, and Subaru *(Love, it's what makes a Subaru, a Subaru)*. Likewise, the president's political

---

[39] *What is Saturation Advertising?*, Neil Kokemuller, Bizfluent, September 26, 2017

"advertising campaign" is continuous, and while he does not control in any way how the news media portrays his statements and actions, they do cover him non-stop. It is having an impact, as Flores and Schachter's research shows; because of the saturation, the general population believes his fictitious and untruthful statements just because they are so ubiquitous, even when they may be clearly identified as false.

Examining this through the prism of advocacy, it's called "The Big Lie."[40] Wikipedia reports it was coined by Adolf Hitler and published in his 1925 book *Mein Kampf*, about a lie so colossal that basically, no one would possibly make that up and therefore it must be true. Few people believe they can get away with such lying, so it's not often done. Professional fact checkers such as Politifact exist to expose liars. Political liars are usually publicly shamed and subsequently shut down from civic debate as a result. But there are no defined rules in the world of public opinion. In October 2018 Politifact reported that only 17% of President Trump's statements as president were "true or mostly true," and they assert that an astounding 70% of his statements are "completely or mostly false."[41] *The Washington Post* has reported similar statistics on the inaccuracy, deception and falseness of President Trump's statements, saying he has made false or misleading claims, and

---

[40] Wikipedia: *Big Lie*

[41] politifact.com/personalities/donald-trump, October 28, 2018

repeated them, more than 10,000 times.[42, 43]

ABC News Reporter Jonathan Karl asked President Trump if he has kept his 2016 campaign promise, where he said "I will never lie to you."[44, 45, 46] In response to Karl in 2018, Trump said "I do try, and I always *want* to tell the truth. When I can, I tell the truth."

"I always *like* to be truthful," Trump added.

Even Trump's former (and short-tenured) White House communications director Anthony Scaramucci, said Trump "is a liar," and that he "should probably dial down the lying."

Nevertheless, President Trump has a very loud megaphone and with relish and enthusiasm bullies people and groups, and manipulates the public, with such misleading propaganda.

This consistent pattern of Trump's falsehoods reminds us of the question before us: **Are these techniques, lying and bullying, successful methods for connecting with the people to achieve effectiveness and get something done together?** As I wrote earlier, occasionally there may be a place for it. Sometimes you must fight fire with fire. It could also be justified by some as Machiavellian, where the ends justify the means. That is, the president so badly wants a

---

[42] In 828 days of his presidency, President Trump has made 10,111 false or misleading claims, an average of more than eight lies per day. Washington Post Fact Checker: Glenn Kessler, Salvador Rizzo, and Meg Kelly, April 29, 2019

[43] The Washington Post counts multiple retellings of the same false/misleading claim, whereas Politifact counts the same statement only once, even when spoken multiple times. Politifact's count in the same time frame is 461 of 658 statements were false/ misleading, with the same percentage as the Post, 70%. Adding in "half-truths," the number of misleading statements rises to 84%.

[44] *Trump: 'When I Can, I Tell the Truth,'* Devan Cole, CNN, November 1, 2018

[45] *Trump Defends Military Presence on Border and Says 'I Do Try' to Tell the Truth,* Jonathan Karl, Devin Dwyer, and Meghan Keneally, ABC News, November 1, 2018

[46] President Donald J. Trump, Campaign Rally in North Carolina, August 2016

tax cut, a change to health care law, to appoint a Supreme Court justice, or even just rile up his base of supporters, he uses any means possible, including lying. In these cases, he may rationalize that it is appropriate to do whatever it takes, including dishonesty, to vilify his opponents and get what he wants. However, I strongly assert that in most situations, such behavior is rarely an effective way to connect with people with whom we want to work and achieve success, particularly those individuals and groups we need to develop a long-term, win-win relationship.

Lukensmeyer's research has shown that about 10% on the extreme left and right—20% total—are not interested in compromise. That leaves 80% of people who have the capacity and interest, given the full range of facts about a situation, to understand the bigger picture. These individuals find they like people with different perspectives, and most important, they can work well together. "That's the hope of how we get out of where we are today," said Lukensmeyer.

Facts, Fake News, and the Impact on Connecting

When seeking to connect with someone, it's important to develop trust in each other. Trust can be defined many ways. I think about it this way: You say what you mean, you mean what you say, and your handshake is a contract. Trust is a bond between two people who seek to develop win-win solutions, and not outcomes where one person wins and the other loses.

Trust, it turns out, hinges on belief. Is your conversation partner someone you can believe? Do they tell the truth? Do they give you the whole story, both pros and cons? Are their facts verified or just based on rumors? Do they ignore facts that don't support their position?

In the era of Donald Trump, there has been a lot of discussion about "fake news." President Trump is fond of using this phrase when he hears something that he believes is either untrue or is information that he and others don't like, is unflattering, or wants to hide. Calling something fake news is equivalent to saying it's a lie, and furthermore, insinuating that the source of the information—the person or organization who said or wrote it—is a liar. It's an effort to discredit the information, and the source, and get others to pay less attention to it.

Interestingly, fake news is not really about what is true or false. It's actually about partisanship.[47] We tend to trust people who have similar beliefs to our own, and we distrust those who have the opposite viewpoint. Likewise, we trust leaders we believe in. Subsequently, when *our* leaders say something about a subject we know little about, because we have given them our trust, we stand firmly behind them, and unquestioningly support their arguments and positions.

Partisanship is like a prism, reflecting an image through glass in different ways to different people. We have a set of beliefs that emanate from labels that may be at our core: Republican. Democrat. Christian. Jewish. Muslim. White.

---

[47] *The Real Story About Fake News Is Partisanship*, Amanda Taub, The New York Times (The Upshot), January 11, 2017

African-American. Mexican. Gay. Straight. For each of these labels, we might imagine a set of beliefs that particular group might have. Doing so is an assumption, of course, and perhaps a wrong assumption, but we do it all the time. The common term is "tribalism."

Tribalism leads to seeking our team—our tribe—winning and their team losing.

We need to be aware of our tribalism, as well as that of others, so we can understand our own thinking and seek to achieve a positive outcome.

We must be aware of the impact of partisanship and tribalism and guard against them unduly influencing our opportunities for successful connection. We don't always know what someone's perspective or motivation is. Rather than trying to change your partner's mind, start by trying to understand their perspective. Remember, your goal on the job is to work together and accomplish something, not necessarily to make a friend for life. You are colleagues. Focus on the opportunity to connect and build what is in front of you. For example, instead of engaging in a hot-tempered debate about Trump vs. Obama, Hillary or the next election, diffuse it. Avoid it. Don't take the bait. Turn the topic toward accomplishing the result of your joint mission.

How do you refocus attention? For example, say "Yeah, I heard that too. That's interesting. What we need to do, however, is focus on accomplishing X."

This is called source credibility. We need to be aware of this blind trust and guard against being a lemming for every issue. Trump is the leader of one tribe. His followers believe him and nearly everything he says. The same is true for Obama. It's a vicious cycle. But understanding this phenomenon leads to addressing it and connecting despite it.

Rather than try to get someone to walk a mile in your shoes, it's best to focus your efforts on the issue in front of both of you.

Arthur C. Brooks, president of the conservative American Enterprise Institute, has a slightly different perspective on the problem and solution.[48] He says the issue is contempt, where each side has anger and disgust not only for each other's ideas, but also for each other. The reasons are the usual suspects: divisive political leaders, talking heads on cable television, angry, hateful activists and columnists, and social media. It's the one-sided arguments we've grown accustomed to, and in our tribal minds, enjoy. Brooks says that contempt makes compromise and progress extremely difficult.

Brooks' solution is to disagree better. Ignore the shouting haters in the media and instead reach out to others and listen to them. Rather than be filled with anger and bile, try to bring a positive attitude. You may still disagree with someone, but do so with compassion. Brooks says we need to uplift and unite, not denigrate and divide, and declares he is devoting the remainder of his career to bringing people together.

---

[48] *Our Culture of Contempt,* Arthur C. Brooks, The New York Times, March 2, 2019. He is the author of the book: *Love Your Enemies: How Decent People Can Save America From the Culture of Contempt*

Leaders Can Lead Us Astray—If We Let Them

—————————— 〝 ——————————

Words do matter. People do listen. When our leaders lower the standards for civility and behavior, all the rest of us feel like we're entitled to do the same thing." [49]

Jeh Johnson, Former Secretary
U.S. Department of Homeland Security

In Albertville, Alabama, an anti-immigration backlash took place in 2007 that is a valuable lesson on cause, effect, and solution. The lessons are similar to backlashes in Europe and elsewhere across the world.[50] This story is based on in-depth reporting by *This American Life*, over an eight-month period talking with more than 100 people.[51]

In a nutshell, immigration was blamed for Mexicans coming to Albertville and taking jobs away from the white townspeople. What actually happened were several actions nearly simultaneously—a weakened labor market, methamphetamine and opioid addiction rates jumping among the local population, and together this synergy sending the crime rate higher.

Albertville residents used to find a modest level of prosperity working at a poultry processing plant. But with these

---

[49] Jeh Johnson, Former Secretary of the U.S. Department of Homeland Security, speaking to Stephanie Ruhle, MSNBC, March 19, 2019

[50] *Where Do Anti-Immigrant Backlashes Come From?*, Max Fisher and Amanda Taub, The Interpreter, The New York Times, August 17, 2018

[51] *Our Town, Parts One and Two*, Miki Meek and Ira Glass, This American Life, Shows 632 and 633, December 8 and 15, 2017

changes, they became poorer, work was scarce, and their community was less safe. Randomly, this happened at the same time migrants came to work at the poultry factories. Immigration seemed like an easy scapegoat.

But it wasn't—at least at first. Initially, people saw the facts and recognized the situation. But then a handful of local politicians—and one national leader, the U.S. Senator from Alabama (at the time) Jeff Sessions—got on the bandwagon and blamed immigration.

The politicians, these so-called "leaders," gave the town's residents a focal point, a place to direct their anger. They characterized the migrants as a threat to the community's economy and safety. They created an "us versus them" mentality, which can be highly motivational to get people to act. Social scientists call this "identity threat," where we see a particular demographic "out-group" as threatening to our existence. As the "in-group," we are inspired to fight back.

Politicians promoting the false threat were elected to leadership positions in town and imposed harsh anti-immigration ordinances. The Alabama legislature took notice of the goings-on in Alberville, and soon thereafter approved similar laws at the state level.

That's brings us to lesson number one from this story: Misguided groupthink takes place not from the bottom up, but from the top down. Even though the links to the problems were weak, leaders blamed immigration in an effort to blame someone—anyone—but not themselves, not local economic circumstances, and certainly not the local drug epidemic.

However, a different dynamic was also taking place in Albertville. The school system was integrating the migrant children in all classes, bringing kids, and ultimately, their parents together. Adults were talking, working together, and getting along. In the school system, from the bottom up, people were feeling that immigration was actually benefitting the community.

Social norms changed over time, and the town elected new leadership who chose to follow the school district model. The immigration backlash subsided, and now it's a thing of the past.

Lesson number two is the power of the bottom-up and understanding clearly what is actually going on in society. We have to be aware of what leaders are saying and also think independently about what's actually going on in order to create the appropriate fixes to society's real problems. Then it's vital to question authority and force them to recognize reality. It's not easy to stand up, but with facts on your side, it's important to make sure decisions are made based on reality rather than fear.

Could Civility Harm Debate?

On August 11-12, 2017, there was a protest in Charlottesville, Va., where people who self-identified as far-right, alt-right, neo-fascists, and white nationalists marched, principally, to oppose removing a statue of Confederate General Robert E. Lee from Charlottesville's Lee Park.[52] There were also counter protests. In the confrontation, one woman was killed and many were injured when a vehicle drove into the crowd of counter-protesters. The entire

[52] Wikipedia: *Unite the Right Rally.* White nationalism was also considered to be a motivation of the protesters.

experience created a high degree of animosity and emotion in the community (as well as receiving significant national attention).

For more than a year in the aftermath, civic leaders heard from the public to find a way forward that would strengthen the community.

Mayor Mike Signer tried to bring people together. However, he didn't know how to allow people to express their strong emotions while simultaneously running the local government. Mayor Signer chose to enforce the standard meeting guidelines of Robert's Rules of Order, as well as adding rules for limiting the length individuals could speak at city council meetings. He enforced prohibitions on heckling, harassment and foul language. Effectively, he tried to impose civility.[53]

It didn't work. Jalane Schmidt, a local citizen and activist, complained that "civility" was being used to shut down the conversation. She argued that because people could not express their opinions publicly, in a sort of non-civil, even disrespectful way, that the deep hurt some felt could not be conveyed in a way that was meaningful to them personally. She suggested it would be the only way to present the passion and get the attention necessary for change to take place.

The concept of civility as a constructive vehicle for public discourse was disputed. This experience suggests that sometimes the only way to get to a calm, civil conversation is first for people to be heard and to say what they feel needs

---

[53] *'Hear Me by Any Means Necessary': Charlottesville Is Forced to Redefine Civility*, National Public Radio, Morning Edition, Debbie Elliott, March 20, 2019

to be said, however they want to say it, and no matter who is offended.

How DARE You Agree with Me![54]

This is a weird one.

Two economists, Christopher Blattman and Stefan Dercon, conducted important research about the opportunity to escape poverty by moving from an agricultural to industrial job.[55] This was ground-breaking research, done in Ethiopia, where such an analysis could be studied because industrialization was taking place for the first time, new factories were being built and were drawing interest from people in rural areas.

Blattman and Dercon postulated what has been economic textbook theory for years: that factory jobs are a stairway out of poverty. What they found, however, was the opposite. They followed about 950 applicants for factory employment over one year who both were and were not offered jobs. Surprisingly, most people quit their industrial job within the first few months, and ended going back to the family farm or working in their original rural area.

It was a wise decision for the employees. They earned about the same pay, but the industrial job turned out to be more dangerous, longer hours, and worse conditions compared to their rural positions. There are many reasons why returning to the rural job was better, but that's not the point of the story.

---

[54] *How DARE You Agree With Me, Sir!*, Max Fisher and Amanda Taub, The Interpreter Blog, New York Times, May 5, 2017

[55] *Everything We Knew About Sweatshops Was Wrong,* Christopher Blattman and Stefan Dercon, The New York Times, April 27, 2017

When Blattman and Dercon published a summary of their work in *The New York Times*, they were attacked by a substantial number of left-leaning commenters who wrote on the *Times'* website. The critical writers didn't question the research results—they agreed with the conclusion that industrialization was bad and the family farm was good. What made them angry with Blattman and Dercon was that the economists had even studied the topic in the first place. Of course, people declared, industrialization is bad. They should have known that from the start. The fact that the economists had carefully put the theory to the test, *and found the opposite result,* had no impact. The fact that the researchers changed their minds about the value of rural vs. factory jobs was meaningless. By taking the opposite position in the first place—that factory jobs might be good—Blattman and Dercon "convinced" their detractors they were on the wrong "team," the other team, the right-leaning conservative one. Changing their minds, and concluding their hypothesis was incorrect, had no impact.

What this experience teaches is that people are quick to take sides, then hold on to their weakly justified viewpoints. This is why it's hard for people with different perspectives to have honest conversations about controversial societal issues, such as universal health care, taxes, abortion, LGBTQ rights, and so on down the list of topics that separate the right from the left.

Why We Deceive Ourselves
and How to Change

"I've long believed that humans are rational beings. That is to say, people use logic and evidence to make decisions and determine what's true. As it turns out, a wealth of cognitive research proves I was decidedly wrong." So writes Mike Fishbein, digital marketer, in *The Science Behind Why Your Facebook Friends Ignore Facts.*[56]

We live in a world where we are flooded with more information than ever before in the history of humanity. Here are just a few communications platforms: TV, the internet, social media, Google, taxicab TV, gas-pump TV, electronic billboards, podcasts, Netflix, Hulu, Amazon, Apple, Stitcher and Pandora radio. To deal with this flood of information, our brains must filter out the noise and interpret the onslaught into something usable, or we'd be overwhelmed. Our brains use shortcuts to pick out bits of information we think are useful. Useful, perhaps, but not necessarily true.

Here's how our brains deal with the information overload and push us toward biases that prevent us from understanding the facts of a situation:

1. We believe what is <u>top of mind</u>. We tend to believe what we already know, can recall easily, and as a result, will likely predict what we think will happen in the future. The stock market falls? Oh no, it's going to fall forever! Pull out all your money from the stock market! Relying on what is top of mind helps

---

[56] *The Science Behind Why Your Facebook Friends Ignore Facts,* Mike Fishbein, October 17, 2016, medium.com

us use our knowledge, our "street smarts." We read, we watch, we post, we follow, and we think we have a complete idea of what's out there. However, even though something is top of mind, that doesn't mean it's true. We must force ourselves to research more and question what we know. Mark Twain said, "It ain't what you don't know that gets you in trouble. It's what you know for sure that just ain't so."[57]

2. Attention bias is our tendency to reach a conclusion based on our recurring thoughts. It's the concept of thinking you know the whole story when you don't. To develop a position, you need to recognize there are things you don't see, and you have to accurately go out and research more information. You've seen this if you have ever known an issue deeply that was written about in a blog, news media article, or appeared in a television or video news report. Usually only part of the story is covered, yet the reporter thinks they are presenting a description of the full story.

3. Repetition is one of the most dangerous and effective methods for leading us astray in believing what's not true. Repeated statements are easier to process and perceived to be more truthful than newer statements. This is why when fast food companies roll out a new product, like a giant hamburger with bacon and a fried egg, and suddenly, we see their advertising everywhere. It's a marketing technique called saturation advertising, whereby all media channels

---

[57] quoteinvestigator.com

are flooded simultaneously with the same message. Repetition makes the thing we see more desirable and a direction we should move in. This is how both effective advertising and advocacy work. "New and Improved!" even when the change is minor. It's also why President Trump in the 2016 presidential election was successful using phrases like "Crooked Hillary," "Little Mario," "Boring Jeb," "Lyin' Ted," and in the 2020 campaign, "Sleepy Joe." He repeats these "bumper-sticker" phrases frequently enough that people tend to shape their opinion of the candidates simply because they hear it repeatedly.

4. Exposure, like repetition, moves us in the direction not only of believing what we hear, but also to have a favorable opinion of it. Because it is familiar, it becomes easier to process, and we understand it better and accept it more easily.

If we want to be an honest broker, someone who has an open mind and does what's right, we must fight these tendencies. It's very, very difficult, and it's easy to fall prey. Knowing how the mind works and how influence can be used and manipulated, we need to dig deeper and seek the truth. This allows us to connect better with others, our primary goal. Understanding the ingredients of deception will allow you to avoid common traps and lead to successfully connecting with your colleagues.

At a forum for the bipartisan citizens' group Better Angels, panelist Howard Weaver noted four methods to help find the truth in today's society.[58] First, there's <u>algorithmic truth</u>. Search a topic online and you're bound to find information that leads you toward what's correct. Second is <u>reputation truth</u>. Do you believe the person conveying the information is a "straight arrow" and does their homework to find the facts? Third is <u>crowd-sourced</u> truth. Wikipedia is a good example, where everyone gets to review and make changes. Over time, the information leans toward the truth. And finally, there's <u>transparency</u>. If a reporter does a lengthy interview and uses just a single quote, it's best to post the entire unedited interview and let the public see everything that was said to determine if any statements were used out of context. Using these methods, it's possible to narrow opinion and get to the truth faster.

The Need to Move Beyond Tribal Politics

―――――――――― 66 ――――――――――

People will generally accept facts as truth only if the facts agree with what they already believe.[59]

Andy Rooney, Humorist
and Television Commentator

A big part of society's inability to come together to address our differences is tribalism and its unconscious impact

---

[58] Howard Weaver, retired Vice President, McClatchy Co., at Better Angels Forum on the Media's Role in Polarizing America, Trinity Cathedral, Sacramento, Calif., October 27, 2018

[59] *brainyquote.com*

on our everyday lives. Jonathan Haidt has written extensively on this issue and offers ideas on how we can move past our differences and work better together. In a nutshell, the solution is: Have a conversation.

Tribalism in the political world has been rising since the late 1990s. It's not just being a member of a political party. This partisan identification is an all-encompassing identity that outweighs any particular policies. And it stems from the core; it becomes people's idea of who they are.[60] Tribalism is now at a point where more than 40% in each party sees the policies of the other party as "so misguided that they threaten the nation's well-being."[61]

The tribal mind, as Haidt and Iyer call it, is full of hypocrisy. Through motivated reasoning, we accept scandalous revelations about our candidate for office and scream bloody murder about the same behavior in their competitor. Social media, sometimes with questionable memes and fake news, only reinforces this perspective. In the past we might have seen ads during the campaign season to influence us. Today, we receive a constant barrage of messages, 24/7, with one-sided opinions and news that leans toward each end of the political spectrum (e.g., MSNBC and Fox News). These fringe-amplified messages reinforce what we think we know already—we're right, they're wrong.[62] We may even go so

[60] *Why Americans Vote 'Against Their Interest': Partisanship,* Amanda Taub, The New York Times, April 12, 2017

[61] *How to Get Beyond Our Tribal Politics,* Jonathan Haidt and Ravi Iyer, The Wall Street Journal, November 4, 2016

[62] Research suggests it's only the fringe 20% (10% on either end of the political spectrum) that is polarized. However, because their public statements are amplified in the partisan media, it appears as if polarization is greater than most people believe. *Is America Hopelessly Polarized, or Just Allergic to Politics?,* Samara Klar, Yanna Krupnikov, and John Barry Ryan, The New York Times, April 12, 2019

far as to believe anyone who supports the other side is an idiot.

Furthermore, we've created a zero-compromise philosophy among partisans—representing their base coalitions—where the perception is "if-they-win-then-we-lose." Today we're actually "more divided around identities than we are around policies," claims New York University professor Kwame Anthony Appiah.[63] "If we just stop using our identity divides we could probably come to reasonable consensus on a whole bunch of things, like immigration, where there's sensible middle ground, but it's not available to us because the people who are most engaged in politics think that every concession is not coming together, but losing to the other side. I think we can talk more about actual policies. Democracy needs the capacity for compromise, and turning everything into an identify issue makes it very hard to compromise."

This is basically a zombie brain, says Rollins College philosophy professor Eric Smaw.[64] It is "zoning out" and doing things unconsciously, where the unevolved brain takes over—the reptilian, mindless part of the brain. It's like driving down the highway on mental autopilot, where we don't think about what we're doing or even remember how we got where we are on the stretch or road. Conversely, freedom, responsibility, and thoughtfulness stem from the evolved brain, the thinking part of the brain. And before you imagine that the *other side* are the zombies, recognize that if you are a strong partisan on either side, *you* may be a political zombie.

---

[63] *The Role of Identity in Politics,* Weekend Edition Sunday, National Public Radio, October 21, 2018
[64] *The College Course on Zombies,* Weekend Edition Sunday, National Public Radio, October 21, 2018

Our zombie minds are often triggered, depending on our beliefs, by words that either support or contradict our opinions and can easily create a physical response, either positive or negative. Generally, the response we are most aware of is the negative one. The positive response just feels normal. We feel good. But a negative word can get your blood boiling. Don't believe it? Read the following trigger words[65] and try to recognize which ones make you feel negative or positive.

Trigger Words

Gun Control	Breitbart
Second Amendment Rights	#MeToo Movement
NRA	Men's Rights Activists
Woman's Right to Choose	Sean Hannity
Pro-choice	Rachael Maddow
Pro-Life	Patriot
Pro-Abortion	MSNBC
New York Times	Fake News
Mainstream Media	Illegal Immigrants
Fox News	American
Democrat	Republican
Liberal Elite	Working Class
White Nationalist	Nationalism
Christians	Muslims
Jews	Unions
The One Percent	Capitalism
Socialism	Taxes
Reverse Discrimination	The War on Christmas
Affirmative Action	Nancy Pelosi
Fascist	Social Justice
Donald Trump	Hilary Clinton
Mitch McConnell	Bernie Sanders
Camouflage Jacket	Confederate Flag
Rainbow Flag	Border Wall

---

[65] *A Guide to Escaping a Politically Feisty Holiday,* Get-It-Done Guy Podcast, Episode 530, December 9, 2018

Interestingly, some of this unconscious one-sidedness may be inherited from our families and the environment in which we grew up, making us to some degree wired toward a particular political philosophy. In an episode of NPR's *Hidden Brain*,[66] host Shankar Vedantam explores this theory with John Hibbing, political scientist at the University of Nebraska-Lincoln. Hibbing talks about "false consensus," where essentially, we believe everyone thinks like us. For example, if we like the color green, we tend to believe that the portion of admirers of green in society is a much higher percentage than it actually is. The same is generally true for things like trucks, sports, opera, warm weather, knitting, foam pillows, and pretty much everything. If we like it, we believe, many people must like it.

Conversely, we think if someone believes the opposite, we are confident they must be crazy.

The explanation, said Hibbing, is in part our upbringing, or heredity. It's what we've grown accustomed to and is influenced by our parents and families. As a result, Hibbing says, it's possible to correlate certain individual characteristics and preferences with political leanings.

Here are a few interesting correlations: Lean left politically, and you'll tend to like ethnic food, multi-cultural music, mixed-breed dogs, and free-form poetry. Lean right, and you like meat and potatoes, music with traditional melodies, pure-bred dogs, and poetry that rhymes. Cambridge Analytica, the right-wing voter profiling firm that hacked into Facebook, found similar correlations, like conservatives

---

[66] *Red Brain, Blue Brain,* Hidden Brain, National Public Radio, October 21, 2018

favor L.L. Bean and Wrangler while liberals prefer fashion from the avant-garde store Opening Ceremony.[67] And researchers from Stanford found similar results in the choices of vehicles: liberals prefer hybrids, while conservatives lean toward pickup trucks.[68]

This heredity correlation is about 30-40%, said Hibbing, which is modest. By comparison, height has a strong 80% correlation being passed along genetically from parent to child. While height is physical and political perspective is intellectual, generally height is not significantly influenced by the environment in which someone is raised, whereas political thought can be.[69]

Okay, so we may be different and it may be *somewhat* hard-wired in our thinking. That's good to know, and it's also good to understand a few of the reasons how we are different and to a degree, why. Thinking optimistically, while this background can explain some of our leanings, a 30-40% parental influence is clearly surmountable.

For the solution, Haidt, Iyer, and others reference Roman philosopher Cicero (63 BC), who observed the solution: proximity.[70] Getting close to people leads to tolerance, particularly, religious tolerance. Getting to know someone from a different political party, race, sexual orientation, or religion

---

[67] *Cambridge Analytica Used Fashion Tastes to Identify Right-Wing Voters,* Vanessa Friedman and Jonah Engel Bromwich, The New York Times, November 29, 2018

[68] *An Artificial Intelligence Algorithm Developed by Stanford Researchers Can Determine a Neighborhood's Political Leanings by Its Cars,* Andrew Myers, Stanford News, November 28, 2017, describing the research of Fei-Fei Li, associate professor of computer science director of the Stanford Artificial Intelligence Lab and the Stanford Vision Lab

[69] Height can be environmentally influenced, and stunted by poor nutrition, for example.

[70] Gibson, William, reviewer (2006). *John Locke, Toleration and Early Enlightenment Culture: Religious Toleration and Arguments for Religious Toleration in Early Modern and Early Enlightenment Europe,* John Marshall, H-Albion

has the impact of diminishing hate and opening minds to perspectives other than our own. The reality is that each "tribe" is generally composed of good people who have important things to say.[71] In fact, people who have a friend or spouse from a different political party are less likely to hate the supporters of that party.

In America, we're losing that proximity. Urban areas tend to be liberal; rural ones and the exurbs lean conservative. Even some churches, where people of all types used to come together and "lay down their swords," have split based on cultural issues such as support or opposition to war, gay marriage and abortion. We need to get proximity back.

Have a conversation, say Haidt and Iyer. Try to develop personal relationships with those on the other side, and understand their arguments. If you know only one side, you don't understand the whole situation. Even just two perspectives may be limited and more voices may be needed. When you do get all the facts, however, you'll not only be better informed, you'll be able to see and consider a variety of options and solutions, not just those from a single perspective.

A powerful technique when conversing with someone on the other side is to point out that you may be wrong about something. Showing your vulnerability is one way to "lower the temperature" of the conversation and be able to discuss a variety of perspectives. Furthermore, your conversation partner may feel motivated to do likewise.

Another option is to praise an action of someone on the other side. Perhaps there is *something* they've said, however

---

[71] *The Righteous Mind, Why Good People are Divided by Politics and Religion,* Jonathan Haidt, p. 366, Vintage Books

small, that is a good idea. It may be the only thing, but by pointing it out, you're suggesting that the thoughts of people who disagree with you have *some* validity. It's a good-faith step in the right direction.

Finally, to truly engage, go back to being curious. Rather than take sides in a way that supports your own opinions, ask why. Why do you feel there's a war on Christmas? What kinds of anti-Christmas actions have you seen? Who has been impacted? Keep going, not being combative, but curious. Say "tell me more." Be so neutral it almost feels like you are on their side. If you do this without sarcasm, hopefully you will find the core of their concern. Then you both can determine what's bugging them. It may be something like seeing a Festivus Pole in a government building next to a nativity scene. With this understanding, you can begin to see the offensiveness they might feel by placing a symbol of a festival initiated by a television comedy, *Seinfeld*, with a holiday that holds significant personal meaning to them.

Our goal is to move from tolerance to acceptance, and then over time, to mutual respect of each other's opinion. We don't have to agree with everyone; however, at a minimum we should recognize the perspective of others as valid.

But Wait! Generation Z Has Needs Too!

———————————— **"** ————————————

Email is a great way to clearly convey basic information. However, when you want to communicate quickly, texting, Facebook and social media can often lead to confusion as information gets left out. If you want to resolve a problem, it's much easier to do so face-to-face. I've seen these communication channels used improperly and lead to major miscommunication.[72]

Lily Moline, Ultimate Frisbee Coach, Seattle

Forget about incivility. There's another vital reason why we need to focus on communication. That is, Generation Z is entering the workforce, and if we want to get work done, we need to examine their communication style. While they come from a plugged-in social media, 33-character tweeting environment, they overwhelmingly want face-to-face communication.[73] And interestingly, email is becoming a burden, perhaps outliving its useful life.

Millennials are those born from 1981-1996, and are firmly in the workplace, eager for advancement. Generation Z (born 1997+) is now entering the workforce, and they have different communication needs. Gen Z is not Millennials magnified, and they don't just want snippets of information on digital devices.

---

[72] Interview with Lily Moline, Ultimate Frisbee Coach, Seattle, August 2016
[73] While the limit for a tweet is officially 280 characters, the average is 33 characters, according to *Twitter's Doubling of Character Count From 140 to 280 Had Little Impact on Length of Tweets,* Sarah Perez, techcrunch.com, October 30, 2018

Yes, Gen Z'ers do look at screens a lot, about twice as much as Baby Boomers.[74] Interestingly, all that screen time has made them hungry for good, old-fashioned face-to-face communication.[75] It's possible that the reason is because people in Gen Z tend to be poor writers, from all that LOLing and emoji/meme communicating. Rather than communicate with the written word, they prefer to talk with their elder bosses, where quite frankly, they both can have the best communication and achieve greater understanding.

The data say 72% of Gen Z prefer communicating face-to-face (including FaceTime, Skype, and Zoom), 9% prefer email, and only 2% want a phone call.[76] There's a lot of communication that can be picked up from seeing someone's face, and Gen Z wants the full sight, sound, and motion to enhance their communications. They also don't want to be talked at; they want two-way communications.[77]

Gen Z wants honesty, integrity, and straightforwardness, even in the face of bad news. They like transparency, because they've grown up in an internet-connected world with the ability to quickly peek behind the curtain and check facts. Authenticity is also key. They believe communication is the most important quality in a leader.

Finally, they want to communicate frequently. For bosses, this means more "management by walking around" and

[74] *Every Generation is Mobile: How Employees Want You to Communicate with Them,* employeechannelinc.com, October 26, 2017

[75] *The Modern Manager's Guide to Communicating with Gen Z Employees,* risepeople. com, May 8, 2018

[76] *72% of Generation Z Want This Communication at Work,* Ryan Jenkins, inc.com, November 8, 2017

[77] *How to Effectively Communicate with Generation Z in the Workplace,* Heather R. Huhman, lab.getapp.com, Nov 15, 2017

chatting with staff, rather than lengthy monthly staff meetings. In other words, check in often. The bottom line is that younger people in the workforce value in-person communication.

Where Does Rudeness Come From? Watch Your Thoughts and Words

There's an expression that is worthy of consideration and inspiration:

———————————— **"** ————————————

Watch your thoughts, they become words;
Watch your words, they become actions;
Watch your actions, they become habits;
Watch your habits, they become character;
Watch your character, for it becomes your destiny.[78]

Frank Outlaw, President of the Bi-Lo Stores

The miscommunication bug bit me in the early days of corporate email. I had a lengthy, two-day, heated debate via email, with Kurt, the guy in the office next to mine. I still shake my head in combined amusement and abhorrence at that unnecessary and inefficient exchange. It's the reason why today I try to limit long, back-and-forth email exchanges. Once I realize that an in-person or telephone conversation would be more efficient, I go to my colleague's office or pick up the phone and call. Email, texting, and social media in general are

---

[78] *What They're Saying,* San Antonio Light, Quote Page 7-B (p. 28), Column 4, San Antonio, Texas. May 18, 1977 (Newspaper Archive)

poor methods for effective communication. They don't fully convey the necessary emotion of a conversation, either humorous, serious, sarcastic, or sad. That happens only when you hear someone's voice or even better, see their face. An often-quoted study—the 55/35/7 formula—suggested that 55% of personal communication is visual (facial and gestures), 35% is tone of voice, and only 7% represents the actual words we use.[79] [80] Seeing and hearing each other is vital to successful communications. While some have suggested that the 55/35/7 split is not precisely accurate and depends on context,[81] I think we can generally agree that interacting with people directly is better for building positive relationships than doing so via email or other forms of electronic communication. We should strive for more direct communication, both in person and on the phone.

In our quest to minimize rudeness and communicate at our best, first we must look inside, train ourselves, and commit to be better.

Recapping the Problem: Incivility and Rudeness Are Increasing, and Communication Methods Are Changing

Incivility and rudeness are on the rise, it's a problem, and it's leading to a culture in both society and the workplace where it is more difficult to collaborate and connect.

[79] Wiener, M., & Mehrabian, A. (1968). *Language within language: Immediacy, A Channel in Verbal Communication.* New York: Appleton-Century-Crofts
[80] Mehrabian, A., & Ferris, S.R. (1967). *Inference of Attitudes from Nonverbal Communication in Two Channels.* Journal of Consulting Psychology, 31, 248-252
[81] Jeff Thompson, PhD, *Is Nonverbal Communication a Numbers Game?, Is Body Language Really Over 90% of How we Communicate?* Psychology Today, September 30, 2011

Unfortunately, working alone and avoiding direct communication tends to be the norm. Furthermore, people and companies are intentionally informing only their side of the story, imposing their biases on the rest of us. Finally, younger employees coming into the workforce desire frequent face-to-face communication. Thus, in order to succeed, we need to change our communication habits.

A lot has been written on the problem of incivility and rudeness, and how it is surging. There's also been good research presented on understanding the psychology of the problem. Some of that is presented here, and if you're interested in more, you can spend a lot of time reading research, reviewing news media summaries, and watching TED talks. Much of it is very good. Unfortunately, less has been written and presented on what works best to fix the problem and get people communicating to work together effectively. That's my goal here—let's get back on the right track.

―――――――――――― **"** ――――――――――――

Watch your words and use them carefully. Whether it's from the pulpit or from the political spectrum, we need to talk to each other and use good words.[82]

Dallas Mayor Mike Rawlings

―――――――――――――――――――――――――――――

[82] Morning Joe, July 8, 2016, in response to the shooting deaths of five Dallas police officers and wounding of seven others

PART 3.
THE POWER OF
PERSONAL STORIES

A nd now, the real conclusion. Rather than wait and hold this until the end of the book, it's important to understand the most important technique people use to connect. Consider this section as a sort of tutorial. Use it and it will improve your relationships and effectiveness.

There is one thread in the case studies that follow, one thing they all have in common: sharing personal stories. The examples show people deliberately interacting and seeking to understand each other as people first, and placing work, or the task-at-hand, second. As a result, they enhance their ability to reach greater understanding and accomplishment on an issue. Many of the cases are quite remarkable. While I encourage you to read them, this section summarizes the main lessons.

While I have also emphasized the need to speak about the same amount of time and assume positive intent, sharing personal stories is the most important trait for connecting.

Share Personal Stories

Here is the "bumper sticker" summary of this book and one of the most important techniques to connect with others: Share Personal Stories.

Get people to tell you about them, and tell people about you. Once you have discussed your backgrounds, you both know enough about each other to achieve a deeper understanding, and can begin to work together on the project in front of you. Sharing personal stories allows both people to open up. That increases comfort, leads to idea development, and expands everyone's ability to consider solutions.

Uchechi Kalu Jacobson runs a software development company in San Francisco. She often brings in new members to her team. "Although we don't all know each other," she said, "telling our stories allows us to understand each person's 'why.' When we share our stories, we are able to have more empathy for the other person and understand their journey."[83]

The Master of Connecting

I have a friend who is a master—no, *the Master*—of conversation and personal connection. He's one of those people who walks into a room and immediately is friends with everyone. I have never seen anyone as good as him in connecting with people. His name is Thomas Tart. We have been friends for years, playing golf, having dinner, and going to sporting events. One day I asked Tom how he did it. How did he connect so easily with everyone he met?

---

[83] *Six Ways to Improve Team Collaboration and Enhance Productivity,* Forbes Community Voice, Young Entrepreneur Council, Contribution from Uchechi Kalu Jacobson, Linking Arts Web Design & Development, forbes.com, June 14, 2018

His answer shocked me. He said, "What are you talking about?"

"Tommy," I implored. "You talk with everyone. You connect with them within one minute of meeting them. Are you telling me you don't notice this?"

"I have no idea what you're talking about, Barry," Tom said.

"Well," I told him. "I'm just going to have to watch and see what you do!"

So I did. I started watching Tom in the interactions he had with strangers. What I found was amazingly simple, and I now use the technique regularly. Here's what he does:

He asks, "Where are you from?"

That's it. This one simple questions leads Tom to one of two next questions. If he knows the place, he'll mention that he has visited there, and engage with his new friend about that place. If he hasn't been there, he'll say, "Wow, I have never been there. Tell me about it!"

And then he listens and engages in conversation. It easily gains momentum from there. People enjoy talking about their hometown, and going deeper, about their journey to get to where they are today. And that's the road Tom takes to get people to engage.

Ask a question and listen for the answer. Contemplate. Respond. Repeat.

The unfortunate thing about listening is that so few people do it. It seems as if the standard for conversation is: You tell me something, I ignore what you say, then I tell you about a similar experience I've had. Rather than continuing to talk about you, now suddenly, we're talking about me.

It might go something like…

ME: How was your weekend?

YOU: Terrible. I wrenched my back picking up a heavy box.

ME: Oh no, what a bummer. Last year I wrenched my back drying my foot after coming out of the shower. I was standing there naked, bent over, and OUCH, my back just seized up. I couldn't even put on my socks. I painfully got dressed, went to the doctor who prescribed these muscle-relaxing pills. Let me tell you about all the side effects...

YOU: (frustrated) I've got work to do… see ya.

Charlie the Shop Teacher

One of my first jobs was as a high school shop teacher in St. Louis. I was green and eager to learn how to be a better teacher. Picture a recent college graduate, age twenty-two, who looks like he's eighteen, standing in front of thirty-five tough kids and expecting to teach them how to use welding equipment, table saws, and about twenty other dangerous tools and machines.

I knew I was inexperienced and wanted to improve. I was in a department of six teachers, most about twice my age. They had much to share, but didn't voluntarily offer much advice. The department chair, Charlie, was a gruff man, the high school's football coach, and highly feared. He walked around his classroom barking orders, and students and his fellow teachers responded with obedient action.

While he wasn't that personable or friendly, he was clearly effective, and I thought this guy had something to teach me.

During the free period in my schedule I sat in his classroom to watch how he managed students. I learned a lot.

Charlie would yell at the kids throughout the class. He called everyone by their last names, which if you're not accustomed to it, can be unsettling. It felt militaristic. In fact, he started class by making students sit in alphabetical order, which they hated, because they preferred to sit with friends. He called roll by last names, and expected a response of "present," or he would record a student as absent.

He'd teach the lesson, and everyone paid attention. Then students would break up around the room to work on projects at the various machines.

And this is where everything changed. Charlie would go up to each student—and he'd get to everyone at least once per week—put his hand on their shoulder, quietly call them by their first name, and ask, "How's it going?"

Students melted. First, they didn't know Charlie even knew their name. But most important, he connected with each of them, so much that they wanted to excel not only for their own growth, but also for him. It's the power of getting personal.

———————————— **"** ————————————

Sharing our stories is in our DNA. On nearly every flight we meet new crew members, and we have to get to know each other quickly and build trust. It's particularly important when you recognize that in an emergency, our lives are in each other's hands.[84]
Linda Roukema, Flight Attendant (retired)

———————

[84] Interview with Linda Roukema, Flight Attendant (retired), May 7, 2019

Personal Stories: How to Get the Ball Rolling

The key to a successful personal conversation is to ask questions and truly listen to the answer, contemplate the response, and continue asking questions. Make the other person the subject. Focus on them. Be curious. Learn about them. Eventually the conversation will turn to you, but for now, imagine you are a talk-show host interviewing a movie star. Say: Hmmm... interesting... wow... really... tell me more....

When you listen, people will enjoy being around you because you make them feel good. When you take this initiative, your relationships will grow, as you are setting the stage for human connection.

―――――――――――― **"** ――――――――――――

We have to get to know each other as people first, because when we do, the likelihood of incivility decreases. When we have a more innate understanding of what makes another person tick, we now have greater respect and are less likely to pass judgement. That doesn't mean we don't disagree, but we can do so with respect. [85]

Bennett Napier, Association Consultant

―――――――――――――――――――――――――

Getting to Know Your Colleagues

Here are some questions you can use to get the ball rolling in your conversations:

―――――――――

[85] Interview with Bennett Napier, Association Consultant, June 2016

- Where did you grow up? Tell me about it.
- When did you move here, and why?
- Where did you work before here? Why did you move away?
- How long have you worked here? How has your job changed?
- Where did you go to school?
- Favorite sports?
- Favorite teams?
- Tell me about your yourself.
- Tell me about your family.
- What activities do you like?
- What are you working on now?
- What has your attention these days?

The Principles of Connecting

In his book *Everyone Communicates, Few Connect*, John C. Maxwell suggests five principles of connection:[86]

- <u>Connecting increases your influence</u>. When you make a connection with someone, you basically have a trusting relationship. This leads both individuals to develop stronger relationships and believe each other. And if you believe in someone, both of you will have a greater tendency to consider each other's ideas and be influenced by them.
- <u>Connecting always focuses on other people</u>. In your interactions, focus on the other person. The more

---

[86] *Everyone Communicates, Few Connect*, John C. Maxwell, Thomas Nelson Books, 2010

attention you pay to them, the more they will enjoy talking with you. As you engage in conversation, mentally assess the time balance of who is talking, and try to lean heavily on them talking, and you being a curious listener. Luciano Pavarotti, the Italian opera singer, once said, "Some singers want the audience to love them. I love the audience." Focus on your conversation partner and they will appreciate you back.

- <u>Connecting goes beyond words</u>. Communicate in a variety of ways if you can. If you are talking in person, be engaged with your facial expressions and the tone of your voice. Empathize with your conversation partner as they tell their story. If you are communicating via email or social media (all poor forms of communication), do your best to show emotion. However you can, express a part of yourself back to them.

- <u>Connecting requires energy</u>. Unless you are a natural connector, make the intentional effort to connect. Recognize that it's going to take some personal effort, particularly if you feel like your normal state of being is not to talk casually with others. I regularly speak before large groups and also have to connect with smaller groups of people I'm trying to influence. I still get anxious about it beforehand. I know that my nervous speedbump is there; it's not a roadblock, and I've had enough experience to know that if I just get the ball going, it'll be okay. I've learned to plow through and connect, and it generally works. Expend the energy, and it'll work for you too.

- <u>Connecting is not a talent but an acquired skill</u>. A few pages ago I mentioned Tom Tart, someone who I think is a master connector. Sometimes before I walk into a room of strangers at a reception, I say to myself: "Be Tom Tart!" It's an amusing personal reminder to take the initiative, introduce myself, be curious, and learn about others. In my life I have not always been able to connect well with people. That's why I researched and practice the skills identified in the first part of this book. Try the ones that speak to you, and your comfort with connecting will grow.

Talking with People Makes YOU Happy

When you engage in a conversation—with a colleague, with a stranger on a train, airplane or elsewhere—*you* become happier.[87] While happiness is not the focus on this book, it's interesting that improving *your* happiness is a really good byproduct. When you reach out to others, you're giving them a "gift"—that is, your time. One of the following cases, in fact, demonstrates this study and shows how in the process of improving your connections to others, you become a happier person.

---

[87] *Mistakenly Seeking Solitude,* Nicholas Epley & Juliana Schroeder, University of Chicago, Journal of Experimental Psychology, July 14, 2014

PART 4.
CASE STUDIES

In the rest of this book, I'll show you true stories where good people found themselves in unusual and in sometimes stressful situations with others. Rather than going at it alone, staying in their silo, they chose to connect. Sometimes they did the opposite of what they believed or felt, but most important, they tried something new, got out of their comfort zone, and in the process, found a connection. Their efforts resulted in profound examples of effectiveness and accomplishment.

The case studies are important, not just because they are good stories, but because we actually need these doses of reality to shift our belief that collaboration actually works. I've already given you several methods to connect well with others; however, you might not act based on what you've read thus far. That's because, as we noted earlier, self-persuasion plays an important role in helping you see the techniques of connecting in action, understanding how others have used them, and then hopefully, trying some yourself.

The movie *The Last King of Scotland* (2006) is based on the true story of Idi Amin, the despicable tyrant of Uganda, and his relationship with his chief advisor, a Scottish doctor. There is a scene in the film where Amin, prone to angry outbursts, complains about the advice his chief advisor recently provided. Against his advisor's recommendation, Amin made the opposite decision (to expel all Asians from the country) and as a result, a crisis ensued. In the scene Amin is angry, and the chief advisor tells Amin that he offered the correct advice (to keep the Asians), but Amin did not follow it. Amin in response says, and I'm paraphrasing, "Yes, you told me, but you did not persuade me!"

Thus far I have told you many things about connecting. We've discussed specific techniques, as well as the communication problems we're seeing in both the workplace and in society, and why it's important to take action to connect with people. Of course, I want to persuade you to act. But as we've already learned, now it's up to you. The goal of the case studies is to show you how others have connected, so you can decide for yourself what will work best for you.

A Young White Nationalist Connected with Friends of Different Cultures and Fought his Roots—and His Family

————————— **"** —————————

Sharing is not an easy thing to do. When you are a little kid it's not easy to share your toys. To share, we have to learn to trust. When we do so, when we communicate, when we're patient and persistent and have a real commitment to make it work, we can be successful at collaborating. [88]

Beth White, Former Director,
The Trust for Public Land, Chicago Office

In many cases where racism exists, the genesis is usually some combination of personal experience as well as influence by others. A person may live in an environment where they see or feel people of another culture receiving some advantage. Sometimes there's also a dose of family "support." That is, parents may have had a negative racial experience in their lives and through their casual discussion at the dinner table or on a family trip in the car, they share their opinions and ideas, the kids overhear, and thus tend to take on the perspective of the people they love and respect. Rarely, however, do parents actually train their children to

[88] Interview with Beth White, Former Director, The Trust for Public Land, Chicago Office, October 2015

be white nationalists. But that's what Derek Black's family did.

Derek Black was a child growing up in the perfect storm of racism. His father started the first white nationalism website, Stormfront. His mother used to be married to David Duke, a former Ku Klux Klan Grand Wizard. And since their divorce was amicable, David Duke became Derek's godfather and had a significant impact on his life.

Derek was homeschooled, so he received a heavy dose of parental influence in racism. He traveled with his father throughout the deep South, attending white nationalist meetings and organizing groups spewing racial and cultural hatred for those who, simply, were not white. As Derek explains it, he didn't believe individuals of a different race were inferior particularly, but rather, the entire culture of that race was inferior. [89] Strange as that may sound, what he's grappling with is his philosophy that there are outliers in every race—people whom he happened to meet and get to know—and *those particular individuals* are different from the people in their general race.

This is a case of strong familial influence. Derek didn't have much personal experience with people of other races; he heard it from his family and read "studies" they gave him "proving" whites were superior.

Derek himself took an influential role in the white nationalist movement and was considered to be an up-and-coming leader. He started a kids' page on the Stormfront website, where he sought to use popular culture references and stories to support white nationalism.

---

[89] The Daily Transcript: Interview with Former White Nationalist Derek Black, The New York Times, nytimes.com, August 22, 2017

Derek's story is long and engaging. The depth of his parents' influence, as well as the experience of growing up around the KKK, might have been a perspective that could be difficult to shake.

And then Derek changed. He went to college.

Derek grew up in South Florida and in 2010 the university he chose to attend was New College in Sarasota. Even though he continued his racial perspective and activities—maintaining the website and even hosting an internet radio show—he started to make friends.

Well, actually, it wasn't that simple. At first Derek led a double life, operating the website and radio show without telling his fellow students and friends. They soon found out and ostracized him. Many wondered, *Who wants to hang out in their dorm room with a white supremacist?*

One student decided to engage, seeking to change Derek, or at least influence him. Matthew Stevenson educated himself on the Stormfront website propaganda and listened to Derek's radio show. Then he approached Derek and asked him to come to dinner.

It wasn't just any dinner; it was a Shabbat dinner, the beginning of the Jewish Sabbath. Matthew hosted regular Shabbat dinners. He was the only Orthodox Jew at the school, so he took it upon himself to cook the Friday night dinners. His guests consisted not only of other Jews, but also people from a variety of races and religions open-minded enough to attend, including Christian, atheist, black, and Latino.

Matthew decided his best shot at changing Derek's thinking was not to confront or ignore him, but rather, to include and engage him. Matthew thought "Maybe he'd never spent time with a Jewish person before."[90]

Derek was a good guest and brought a bottle of wine. And he came back every Friday night for months. No one ever mentioned Stormfront or white nationalism. They did, however, talk about personal experiences, like one guest, a Peruvian immigrant, discussing his experience attending a high school in the U.S. that was majority Latino. They discussed controversial topics like Israel and Palestine. Matthew and Derek, although at first wary of each other, started to like each other. They began playing pool at a bar on campus.

Some members of the Shabbat dinner group also started to interact with Derek, asking his opinion on some controversial topics. He told them he didn't believe in violence, the KKK, Nazism or even white supremacy. He said those issues were different from white nationalism. Basically, he said it was best for all races to live separately, each in their own homeland.

In an example of source credibility, Derek wrote in an email to his Shabbat dinner friends, "I guess I only value the opinions of people I know." He was getting to know people with opinions different from those he grew up with, and because he respected them, he considered their opinions of value.

As his perspective evolved, Derek decided to respond publicly on a New College student message board, also called the Forum. He chose his words carefully, reflecting the experience and people he had encountered at the school.

---

[90] *The White Flight of Derek Black,* The Washington Post, October 15, 2016. Also, while not referenced here, a book has been written about Derek Black's experience: *Rising Out of Hatred, The Awakening of a Former White Nationalist,* Eli Saslow, Penguin Random House, 2018

He wrote that the endpoint of white nationalism wasn't deportation of non-whites, but gradual self-deportation, in which non-whites would leave the U.S. on their own. He also wrote that he didn't believe in self-deportation right now, and not for his friends, and really, only in concept. He said, "I do not support the oppression of anyone because of his or her race, creed, religion, gender, socioeconomic status or anything similar."

In subsequent posts he went further, completely disavowing the white nationalism movement and the belief system of his parents. "The things I have said as well as my actions have been harmful to people of color, people of Jewish descent, activists striving for opportunity and fairness for all. I am sorry for the damage done."

Derek's posts were published on the website of a very public place—the Southern Poverty Law Center—which is at the forefront of fighting racial discrimination.

The post, and several other public exchanges as well where Derek disavowed white nationalism, created a problem for Derek at home. As he has further embraced multi-culturalism, even visiting many countries around the world, he has become distanced from his family and the former life he led.

The scientific principle at work here is called the "Intergroup Contact Theory" of prejudice reduction. This is where the more we know someone different from us, the greater our understanding and lesser our prejudice. Interpersonal contact is one of the most effective ways to reduce prejudice between majority and minority group members.[91]

---

[91] Wikipedia: *Contact Hypothesis*

Today Derek speaks out against white nationalism from the perspective of someone who has followed two different philosophical paths in life.[92] He started in life influenced by a strongly opinionated family that cast a one-sided spell over him. By spending quality time with people of other cultures and opening his mind to ideas different from his, Derek Black showed the value of connecting.

[92] *Why I Left White Nationalism,* R. Derek Black, The New York Times, November 26, 2016

Oil Workers Improve Safety and Production by Learning to Listen

———————— **"** ————————

There's a TED Talk by Yves Morieux about the most common rules at work that keep us from getting things done. [93] These are rules that nearly everyone follows: measurement, accountability and clarity. We hear it daily. But none of them are important. When we focus on those three rules, we are actually focused on the effort of just one, measurement. Employees think "I've got to meet my metrics, so if I have to crush you and make you look bad, I'm going to do it to get my raise or bonus." What we really need is cooperation, and joint goals.[94]
                 Joe Awad, Manager, Colorado Springs

If you need convincing that connecting works, the title of this case study says it all. By learning how to work together, the roughnecks and roustabouts on drill rigs at Shell Oil improved both their safety record and rate of oil production significantly. In other words, they saved lives of their fellow workers while improving the profits of the company.

When I first heard this case study, I was convinced this

---

[93] *How Too Many Rules at Work Keep You from Getting Things Done*, Yves Morieux, TED Talk, June 2015
[94] Interview with Joe Awad, Manager, Colorado Springs, November 2015

book had to be written. There were other motivations to initiate the project, but this is the story that inspired me to commit to research how best to connect and share the ideas. Most significantly, it's one of the few case studies where there's a link between a behavioral change and how connecting with people leads to a quantifiable, positive result.

Conversely, this story may be a little difficult to link its relevance to the typical workplace. Thus, I wondered whether to use it at all. Let's just say this: you don't have to do what Shell Oil did, but if you do something similar, or perhaps use the exercises provided in the first section, I believe you can improve your office teamwork significantly.

One more thing. This Shell Oil story has been told by National Public Radio[95] and others[96] in a certain way—that is, with extreme "touchy-feelyness." For that reason, it's not my kind of workplace story. Therefore, I'm going to share it with you without much of the strong emotion, which has been portrayed mostly of burly blue-collar men weeping. We'll discuss the emotions and how they played a part in connecting, but I want you to fully understand that experiencing strong emotions is not necessary to achieve the same level of success in your organization or life.

People who work on drill rigs are tough. They're rugged, work hard, and they like to get the job done. They are also accustomed to accidents, and because of their dangerous work, they risk death every day.

In 1997, Shell Oil started to build an offshore oil rig.

---

[95] *How Learning to Be Vulnerable Can Make Life Safer*, Invisibilia, National Public Radio, July 17, 2016
[96] *How Making Oil Rig Workers Cry Created an 84% Reduction in Incidents,* Christopher Notley-Smith, Safey Advice, Safety News, donesafe.com

Ursa would stand 48 stories tall, and when completed, would drill the world's deepest offshore well. It was a big project. Shell began assembling the drilling team and knew it wanted this one to be different. They wanted it to be better, safer, and more productive than the typical drill rig in their fleet.

Shell hired a leadership consultant during the construction of Ursa, Claire Nuer, who was tasked with accomplishing those big goals of extreme safety and high productivity, as well as to improve them company-wide. Shell had never worked with Nuer, but she convinced senior officials she could do it. While this is not a central issue to the story, Shell managers actually had no idea how to accomplish the lofty goals set for safety and productivity. Nuer never had worked in this rough environment or with these types of people—in fact, she was French and barely spoke English—but somehow convinced them she was up to the task, and Shell management decided to give her a chance.

Rick Fox was the project manager for Ursa. In his first conversation with Nuer, Fox told her about technical issues, such as drilling schedules, equipment needs, how the project worked, and what was expected of the men. Nuer stopped him and said his real problem was not schedules or equipment, but fear. To improve safety and production, the change she would seek would be how the men dealt with their feelings. (I told you this would be touchy-feely.)

This likely would not be easy, dealing predominantly with tough men, men who don't talk much, are guarded in almost all respects, and have probably been like that much of

their lives. Fox was even less convinced than senior management, but still, let it move forward.

Over the next year and a half, while Ursa was under construction, Nuer and her team put more than a hundred oil
rig workers through seminars and exercises designed to get
them talking with each other.

A lot of the men objected and didn't understand how all
this talking related to oil production. Nevertheless, they participated, and told stories of their lives and families. They
shared stories of good times, bad times, failed relationships,
and alcoholic parents. They put their personal lives out there.
They listened to each other.

At times it got very personal, with people talking about
their own battles with illness and even the death of children.
Few if any knew details about each other's private lives, so
these intimate stories were a surprise to many. Some men
cried. Yet no one called anyone a crybaby.

They paired off and asked each other questions like
"What's the one thing you would change about me?" They
told one man he talked too much and was a poor listener.
Instead of snapping back an insult, he responded using the
technique he had been trained to encourage listening. He
said, "Tell me more."

The men began to better understand both themselves and
each other, and how they could improve their interactions.
A Harvard Business Review study examined the project and
found that as the men improved the understanding of their own
selves, they became better communicators when discussing

work on the oil rig.[97] An important part of working safely involves being able to admit mistakes, being open to learning, and not being afraid of reprimands. People need to get over their vulnerability and perceived weakness when they say, for example, "I need to move this motor. Would you help me?"

Likewise, in an office environment, someone might need to understand how to interpret a financial balance sheet, or the main points of a memo the boss is looking to be written. Employees need to feel comfortable to ask what they might feel are "dumb" questions and know everyone shares the same goal—efficiency (do it once) and effectiveness (do it correctly).

This new way of interacting contributed to an 84% decline in Shell's accident rate companywide. Also, during the same timeframe, Shell's productivity and efficiency exceeded the oil industry's previous benchmark.

Basically, Shell created a new type of oil rig roughneck, one who cares about his fellow worker, and wants them to be safe, successful, and productive.

- They got to know their colleagues by understanding their backgrounds, listening to their interests, and asking questions.
- They regularly shared what was going on in their lives. Whether it was good or bad news, it didn't matter. Most important was the act of sharing and listening.
- And perhaps most important, when someone gave

---

[97] *Unmasking Manly Men*, Robin J. Ely and Debra Meyerson, Harvard Business Review, July-August, 2008

feedback they didn't like hearing, they responded with "Tell me more," in order to put it all on the table.

Quick sidebar on safety: I'm kind of a stickler for safety, having personally worked in industrial settings and had humble mentors who cared about the health of people around them. When I see someone working in an unsafe environment, like a lawn maintenance or construction worker using machinery without safety glasses, I'll stop and ask them if they have safety glasses handy. They almost always do. I don't reprimand or threaten to turn them in for working dangerously. I say something like "You don't know me, but I want you to go home safely to your friends and family. Wearing safety glasses will protect you." My goal, of course, is that they wear the glasses. I also want them to think about others in their lives who care about them and want them to come home without injury. When we know people care, there's a better chance we'll act.

I had a colleague who would say to me (when I might have been careless with my personal protective equipment), "Barry, I love you, man. Let's wear our safety glasses and hard hats today." I heard that not too long ago, about five minutes before a large bolt fell from atop a 30-foot power pole and bounced off my hard-hat-covered head, protecting me from a certain emergency room visit.

The funny thing is that even though telling someone you care sounds a bit odd, especially in the workplace, it's memorable. I think of it often, and that's why I'm telling you this story now—because I want you to make it home safely, and so you can help others do the same.

Google's Quest to Create the Perfect Team

———————— **"** ————————

I can get a lot done by myself, but I get a lot more done when I work with others. And sometimes working with people isn't easy. It's vital to incorporate different perspectives, which we need to have a well-rounded team that considers a lot of ideas and comes to the best solutions.[98]

Danette Scudder,
Senior Executive, Chattanooga, Tenn.

———————————————————————

There's no question that if you have the secret for creating the perfect team, you'll have an advantage that allows your organization to develop excellent outcomes—be they services or products—and achieve them with committed employees. And if you're Google, a company with significant resources for investigating and solving this elusive riddle, you'd take on this responsibility.[99]

Variations on the secret sauce for teamwork have been published in business books for decades. Here's a digest of what several sources say about creating an organizational

[98] Interview with Danette Scudder, Senior Executive, Chattanooga, Tenn., October 2015
[99] This section is based on *What Google Learned From Its Quest to Build the Perfect Team*, Charles Duhigg, The New York Times, February 25, 2016

culture of teamwork:[100]

- Communicate clear expectations.
- Executives must model teamwork behavior with each other and with other departments.
- Talk about the importance and value of teamwork.
- Reward and recognize teamwork.
- Tell stories about how teams have succeeded in the organization.
- Provide feedback that emphasizes teamwork.

And here's the list of what they say about the rules for teamwork:[101]

- Consider each employee's ideas as valuable.
- Be aware of employees' unspoken feelings.
- Act as a harmonizing influence.
- Be clear when communicating.
- Encourage trust and cooperation among employees on your team.
- Facilitate communication.
- Delegate problem-solving tasks to the team.
- Encourage team members to share information.
- Establish team values and goals; evaluate team performance.
- Make sure that you have a clear idea of what you need to accomplish.
- Use consensus.

---

[100] *How to Build a Teamwork Culture in Your Organization,* The Balanced Careers, thebalancecareers.com
[101] *Steps to Building an Effective Team,* Berkeley Human Resources, hr.berkeley.edu

- Set ground rules for the team.
- Establish a method for arriving at a consensus.
- Encourage listening and brainstorming.
- Establish the parameters of consensus-building.

That's a long list, and it is difficult to understand which components, if any, are most important. Google sought to determine those critical elements so they could form effective teams as quickly as possible.

Harvard researchers wondered if putting people together to work in the same large room—an open office environment—improved teamwork and effectiveness. In a study on the value of an open workspace, researchers found that this can lower productivity and connectedness.[102] While physical proximity is important to get to know people, being too close in a work environment can drive people away from direct interaction and toward greater use of email. In the study, employees in open offices spent 73% less time in face-to-face interactions, while email and messaging use increased by more than 67%.[103] When "housed" together in the same large office, people may plug into music devices to limit ambient noise, talking, and other distractions. They seek out ways to concentrate better, and thus increase their email communications. Basically, they move communication from one channel, face to face, to another channel that is electronic. Email, of course, is a poor platform

---

[102] *The impact of the 'open' workspace on human collaboration*, Ethan S. Bernstein and Stephen Turban, Philosophical Transactions of the Royal Society B, Biological Sciences, The Royal Society Publishing, July 2, 2018, Volume 373, Issue 1753, rstb.royalsocietypublishing.org

[103] *Here's the Final Nail in the Coffin of Open Plan Offices*, Libby Sandler, Fast Company, July 19, 2018, fastcompany.com

to advance teamwork. The bottom line from this research is that collaboration declined in an open office environment.

Examining a variety of options to improve teamwork, Google found that the long list of characteristics, however broad or specific, did not produce consistent results. They sought to find what was working in actual teams so they could apply those elements to the many groups of employees they had operating already. At any point in time, Google has more than a hundred teams working on projects, many with uneven results. Ultimately, the company wasn't just interested in solving a societal puzzle for teamwork to share with the world; rather, they wanted better, faster, and cheaper results from their own teams. It was a worthy exercise because they sought to improve the company's effectiveness, productivity, and ultimately, profit.

Google initiated a quest, which they called Project Aristotle, to examine the teams they had across the company, evaluate which were most effective, and determine the factors that made them effective. Note that Google didn't set out to *try* to determine the factors; they were *certain* they could determine them with their exceedingly strong ability to correlate many facets of a problem.

The first hypotheses they had centered around several concepts about how to combine and create the best teams. The found these to be wrong, or at best, inconsistent:

- Combine the best people on a topic, like a team of all-stars.
- Bring together like-minded personalities, such as all-introverted or all-extroverted people in single groups.

- Gender balance, and also, gender imbalance.
- Put people together who:
  - Are friends away from work.
  - Have similar interests.
  - Are motivated by the same kinds of rewards.
  - Have similar education.

After examining 180 teams in 2012, they couldn't find any evidence or correlation of the team composition that made a significant difference in how the best teams functioned. No mix of personalities, skills, or backgrounds made any difference. Nothing seemed to matter.

Some of Google's most effective teams were composed of people who socialized away from work, while others were total strangers outside their meetings. Some effective groups had strong managers leading the way, and others had no hierarchical structure. Even more confusing, some teams had nearly identical compositions but radically different levels of effectiveness. Google, a company expert at finding patterns, couldn't find any strong patterns.

Setting aside the characteristics, skills, and backgrounds of the individuals, Google examined just the behaviors of the individuals on effective teams. They found two elements that produced successful workgroups:

1. No single person dominated the conversation. This isn't to say there were rules about timing how long each person spoke; rather, it just turned out that groups found a balance in the amount of time each person spoke and participated. Basically, they took

turns talking and listening, and were conscientious to give everyone similar time.

2. Everyone had a high degree of emotional intelligence, social sensitivity, and empathy. That is, they were skilled at intuiting how others felt based on their tone of voice, expressions, and gestures. They seemed to know when someone was feeling upset or left out, and then found a way to address those situations directly.

The company did learn that two other sub-elements were also important: establishing clear goals that defined the team's purpose, and making sure everyone was responsible and dependable, engaged in the team, and carrying their weight.

Then Google had to figure out how to take what they'd learned about communication and empathy and scale it up to create other successful teams. What they learned is that group members sharing something on a regular basis about their personal lives, however small or big, is a way to open the door. Some might begin a meeting by talking about what they did over the weekend. Others might talk about a son's or daughter's recent accomplishment. In one case, the team leader told the group he had serious health issues, which was not only deeply personal, but also impactful in connecting with his teammates.

Google found, basically, that we don't like to put on a "work face" when we come to work. Life is messy for all of us. We have ups and downs, successes and failures, and sometimes we wade through boredom. In balancing our work and home lives, we nevertheless want to remain human, talk with others about our lives, desires, experiences, and plans, and also get some good work done to benefit our employer and contribute to society.

In the quest to build the perfect team, Google found that

imperfection may be the key. In other words, the best teams listen to each other and are sensitive to feelings and needs.[104] Today, their efforts have morphed, in one way, to "Coffee Chats," where Google employees are encouraged to meet new colleagues inside the company and learn more about each other.

When our daughter Emily was a toddler, my wife and I visited Virginia Beach for a long weekend. One evening our daughter had a stomach bug that kept her up much of the night. The next morning was rough for us, pretty sleep deprived. We entered the elevator to head to the beach. I don't remember all the details of how it happened, but within seconds my wife became engaged in conversation with another mother—and all others present in the elevator—about Emily's late-night sickness and how tired we were. The other mother was immediately sympathetic, and throughout the 90-second ride down to the lobby, she and my wife bonded. For many years, I joked with my wife about oversharing our personal life in that short elevator ride. And to this day it's still a thing she amazingly does, making quick, personal connections. It turns out she naturally achieves what the best teams do: share what's going on in their lives and build connections.

---

[104] Some disagree with the conclusion of Google's quest to build a perfect team, believing the ingredients are more complex to create well-functioning teams. Burnison reports that another study emphasizes pragmatism as a key characteristic; that is, everyone on the team focusing on the goal to be accomplished. Here I've chosen to emphasize a characteristic I believe is vital: sharing equally. Why? Because I've seen it personally, it exists as a common thread across the case studies, it's backed by research (Equity of Voice) and, quite randomly, much of the results of investigations and interviews for this book. For this contrary discussion of Google's project, see: *7 Years Ago, Google Set Out to Find What Makes the 'Perfect' Team—and What They Found Shocked Other Researchers*, Gary Burnison, CNBC, February 28, 2019.

Bipartisanship Actually Exists in Washington, D.C. and Is Growing in State Legislatures

———————— " ————————

We may never find that common ground with people whose politics or faith conflicts with ours. But we owe it to one another to disagree agreeably, without anger or intimidation, whether on a front porch or a Facebook page. A little more grace among us all would go a long way toward healing the nation.[105]

Erick-Woods Erickson, Conservative Blogger

Some Republicans and Democrats Are Trying to Come Together

For collaboration, one of the most dysfunctional places in the world is the United States Congress. If it were a business, it would be a money loser. If it were a sports team, no one would show up to watch. If it were a couple, they'd be divorced.

"When I first got elected in 2008 one of my best friends was also elected to Congress," said U.S. Representative Tom Rooney (R-FL). "We went through basic training together in the military, and we both were at West Point together. He got elected as a Democrat from Philadelphia, and I've known

---

[105] *How to Find Common Ground,* Erick-Woods Erickson, The New York Times, September 30, 2017

this guy forever. At West Point we used to go to a bar every Thursday night, and so [in D.C.] we said let's go have a beer on Thursday for old times' sake. There were other members of Congress who walked into the bar and gave me the evil eye that I was sitting there drinking with a Democrat."[106]

"The Venn diagram of agreement between Democrats and Republicans used to overlap. Today, they are at opposite ends of the spectrum with no overlap," said Eliot Spitzer, former Governor of New York.[107]

As difficult a problem as this has become, a handful of legislators is trying to change it. They are a group of Democrats and Republicans—more than 40, which is about 10% of the House of Representatives—committed to working together as much as possible.

The Bipartisan Working Group (BPWG) began quietly in 2012 by Rep. John Carney, Democrat of Delaware and Rep. James Renacci, Republican of Ohio. The BPWG's goal is to "pitch ideas, find co-sponsors for initiatives and discover avenues for collaboration across the aisle."[108]

Admission is by invitation only, with members of the group evaluating who would be a good fit. Two must be added simultaneously, one Republican and one Democrat. They meet weekly, and all members must attend at least 75% of the meetings.

BPWG members come from many states and regions, including Pennsylvania, Indiana, Virginia, New York, Texas, California, Michigan, Ohio, Nevada, Maryland, Alabama,

---

[106] *The Daily* Podcast, The New York Times, July 19, 2017
[107] *Real Time with Bill Mahr,* HBO, Season 14, No. 23, July 15, 2016
[108] *The Bipartisan Working Group's Elusive Target,* Emma Dumain, Roll Call, August 11, 2015

Massachusetts, and Illinois. They've worked on a variety of issues and have passed several bills together.

Representative Dan Webster, a Central Florida conservative, described their regular dinners, where the only rule is there must be an even number; that is, everyone has to bring—or be brought by—someone from the other political party.

"At the dinner I am the Republican, said Webster. "Debbie Wasserman Shultz, a friend and [member of Congress] colleague from Florida I've known for 35 years, not quite from the same ilk that I am, is the Democrats' host. The ticket to get in is to bring someone of the opposite party. I once had someone who called to say their person had canceled, can I still come? I told them no, you need another person from the other side.[109]

"When we did the first one," said Webster, "I had Republican members of Congress saying: 'I don't want to be in the same room with her, why would I go to dinner with her?' I said, 'They feel the same way about you!'

"After one dinner," continued Webster, "a legislator who had never reached across the aisle to work with a member of the other party, said it was the best dinner they'd ever been to. What they learned is that people are people. Everyone has interesting stories about how they got to Congress and they all have families. They have many things in common.

"There was a movement several years ago to sit on the floor with a member of the opposite party during the State of the Union Address," said Webster. "That was a big thing.

---

[109] Interview with U.S. Representative Daniel Webster, Orlando, Fla., June 19, 2017

I asked Debbie if she wanted to sit with me—actually, I called three Democrats and I said, 'I'll sit with the first one who calls me back.' She was the first one to call. After the State of the Union we said we've got to get together and figure out a way to bring people in and get them talking with each other. We have to let everyone know that Democrats and Republicans are just people, and everyone has common issues and concerns. It's been very good. However, I don't think the Congressional leadership on either side likes it.

"I have my office in the Longworth House Office Building because there are more Democrats there," said Webster, a Republican. "I started a 'Ground Floor Club.' I went around and met every Member of Congress with an office on the ground floor. I went to Democratic Representative Marcia Fudge's office, from the Cleveland area. The staff didn't know what to do, [and wanted to know] why I was just popping into another Member's office. Marcia came out and said, 'Come on in!' Then she started introducing me to people she knew on the floor of the House. It really helped break the ice. The result is you develop relationships. That's the start. None of Democrats I've ever met through this group have ever trashed me on the floor, and I haven't done anything to them. What happens next is you get the chance to tell your story.

"When I sit down with folks, I ask them 'How did you get here? Why did you run for Congress?' Everybody's got a story, and I ask them to tell their story. Funny thing is, Members of Congress love microphones. We'll make a speech to an empty chamber. We like talking. But when somebody actually listens to you? It just doesn't happen that often. I've learned the power of listening.

"No matter what side they're on, most people run for Congress because they are cause-oriented," said Webster. "They rarely get to tell anyone that. How did I get here? What's my family like. Let me tell you about my grandkids. Everybody who comes into our offices wants something— money, creating a new regulation, stopping a regulation, or something else. And everybody on the floor of the House is in it for themselves. So there's no one to listen to our stories.

"I've found that listening just breaks down the barriers," said Webster.

"

[There is a huge portion of] America that really is crying out for moderation and a lack of divisiveness and civility and cooperation and bipartisanship."[110]
                    Governor Larry Hogan (R-Maryland)

The Problem Solvers Caucus and No Labels are Leading Important Bipartisan Changes

The Problem Solvers Caucus is a durable, bipartisan bloc in Congress committed to getting to "yes" on key issues. The caucus evolved in 2017 out of the grassroots organization No Labels, which has been working since 2010 to build

---

[110] *Can Larry Hogan Save the Republicans?,* Frank Bruni, The New York Times, August 5, 2018

bridges over the gulf separating Democrats and Republicans on key issues. [111] No Labels was started by Nancy Jacobson, a political Independent with many years of experience in gubernatorial, senate, and presidential campaigns. No Labels has championed ideas designed to put problem solving above politics.[112] The group seeks to bring political leaders together to address tough problems, with the goal to make government work for the people. They are not a third political party, but rather, a voting bloc advocating for good ideas, and unity. The organization is large and has a broad reach, with more than a million members across the country engaged and informed in its activities.[113, 114]

No Labels believes the far right and far left are holding America hostage, growing evermore strident, and making effective governance increasingly difficult. While those fringe groups tend to be small on either end of the political spectrum, they are organized, they vote and are engaged in campaigns. On the contrary, the larger political middle cringes at such showmanship—and unfortunately—often stays on the sidelines in campaigns, and may even be less inspired to get out and vote.

In 2017, with the help of No Labels, two members of the U.S. House of Representatives got together to create the bipartisan Problem Solvers Caucus. Reps. Josh Gottheimer (D-NJ) and Tom Reid (R-NY) formed the caucus to seek bipartisan fixes on the biggest problems dividing the nation. In

---

[111] This section relies heavily on the website for the group "No Labels," nolabels.org

[112] Wikipedia: *Nancy Jacobson*

[113] *The Future of the American Center,* David Brooks, The New York Times, November 29, 2016

[114] No Labels has a $4-5 million annual budget with 15 staff, and will expand during the upcoming election with additional field organizers

2018 it had 48 members, equally split between Republicans and Democrats.

The Problem Solvers Caucus has developed bipartisan policy ideas, including proposals to address health care, gun safety, infrastructure, and immigration/border security. Because House rules are controlled by the majority party, the caucus noted the rules prevented their bills from being considered on the House floor. They worked with Speaker Nancy Pelosi and were successful at getting the rules changed in the 2019-2020 Congress to allow bipartisan proposals to come to the floor for consideration.

While bipartisanship brings people and ideas together to address problems, the reality is that partisans do not want problems to be solved. As we've seen earlier, the continuance of tribal politics depends on groups *not* finding solutions, *not* liking each other's ideas, *not* liking each other, and ultimately, thinking the other side is just plain stupid, or in the worst case, evil.

In politics, the problem of bipartisanship starts in the primaries. Voters in Democratic and Republican primaries are the most partisan, and candidates tend to move further left or right in the primaries. As candidates lean toward the fringes in those elections, each party's winner advances to the general election intending to promote their side's positions. Historically, there has been little benefit to being bipartisan in a primary election. And in the general election, there's has not even much of a bipartisan voter presence, as liberals and conservatives tend to dominate the messaging.

No Labels seeks to change that. An important element of their mission centers on citizens' action and the organization's commitment to combatting the influence of divisive primary campaigns. When Democratic leaders live in constant fear of challenges from the far left and Republican leaders live in constant fear of challenges from the far right, all the incentives point leaders away from bipartisan problem solving. But if citizens get involved, organizing in support of bipartisan leaders and standing up for them in primary elections, new possibilities can emerge for progress. In that spirit, No Labels works actively to promote the grassroots, and to steer support for problem solvers on both sides of the aisle.[115]

The road ahead may appear long and uphill. But No Labels is developing a viable counterweight to the political impulse toward tribalism. A decade ago, few could have imagined the Problem Solvers Caucus would have such influence, or that No Labels would be the thriving grassroots organization it has become.[116] The organization has also produced a series of books identifying issues both sides want to address. In the *No Labels Policy Playbook*, they provide 60 ideas in four main areas: jobs, social security and Medicare, budget and energy. They are taking an active role during the 2020 presidential election, holding a large Unity Convention in New Hampshire. It will include a candidate forum to discuss the value of bipartisanship on issues both sides want to address. It is sure to get attention.[117]

The cliché is correct: You gotta have a dream if you want to make a dream come true,[118] and No Labels is making

---

[115] nolabels.org/history-3
[116] Ibid
[117] Interview with Ryan Clancy, Chief Strategist, No Labels, April 2019
[118] Oscar Hammerstein II, brainyquote.com

significant progress to deliver on that dream, engaging constructively with those who want to solve problems.

———————— " ————————

When people disagree, I don't like them saying "You're wrong." That puts others on the defensive. I encourage them to say "That's interesting. My experience has been different, let me share it with you."[119]
Lt. Col. (Ret.) Jill Morganthaler

Bipartisanship Is Growing in a Few State Legislatures

Recognizing that 50% of Congress served in their state's legislature before running for higher office, the National Institute for Civil Discourse (NICD) is trying to set the stage early in the arc of state politicians' careers to have an impact now and also later, in Congress. NICD is a nonpartisan organization that combines research and practice to address political dysfunction and advocate for civility in governance through three target areas: elected officials, the media, and the public.[120]

NCID holds half-day workshops around the country for state legislatures titled "Building Trust Through Civil Discourse." They are co-facilitated by a Republican and Democratic legislator in the state where the workshop takes place. Their mission is to provide legislators with an

---

[119] Interview with Lt. Col. (Ret.) Jill Morganthaler, November 2015
[120] nicd.arizona.edu

opportunity to explore the benefits of improving the level of civil discourse in their state's legislature and more effectively work across the aisle.

As of 2018, they've held 23 workshops in 16 states, reaching more than 750 state legislators. Many state legislatures now incorporate the workshop into new-legislator orientation programs, and training is scheduled through 2019.[121]

The foundation of the effort began when Ted Celeste decided to run for the Ohio Legislature in 2006. Because of his involvement in his church's effort to improve political discourse, Celeste decided to run a positive campaign for the state legislature. It was tough, especially when he was under attack by his opponent. But he persisted and beat the incumbent.[122]

His first day in the Ohio Legislature the Democratic Caucus met. He was told "You're going to hear requests from the other side to work with them. Don't talk to them, don't believe them, they are the enemy."

Celeste ignored that advice and sought out Republican colleagues when he started working on the bipartisan issue of increasing funding for the teaching of dyslexic children. His own Democratic leadership refused to pass the bill only because he had a Republican co-sponsor. They told Celeste, "You're not going to introduce that bill because the election is coming up and we don't want people thinking Republicans care." Enough Democrats lost in that Ohio election that they also lost control of the House. In the next legislative session

---

[121] *Levels of Discourse, Teaching Civility Across the Aisle One state at a Time,* Ted Celeste, Worldview Magazine, pp 12-13, Vol. 31, No. 4, Winter 2018
[122] Interview with Ted Celeste, July 7, 2016

Republicans were in charge. They introduced the same legislation, and Celeste, along with Republican legislators, passed the bipartisan bill on dyslexia.

With that experience under his belt, Celeste decided to pull together a meeting of people interested in making a difference and improve civility and culture. NCID, which had been recently formed, decided to take on the effort.

As Celeste describes it, there are three vital elements to breaking down barriers and begin the conversation:

1. Share a meal. People relax and share details about their personal lives more easily when they "break bread."
2. Establish ground rules. The group decides the type of civil conversation they want to have, then they stay within those boundaries of respect for each other.
3. Discuss their personal journey. The goal is for each person to think about events in their lives that had a profound impact on establishing their values and who they are personally. This leads to describing the foundation and shaping of their personality, as well as understanding what inspires them.

In the Personal Journey exercise, participants write those major events on sticky notes, then place them on a timeline on the wall. Each legislator then takes their turn walking the group through their major life's events. They also learn that their motivation to serve the public is frequently similar, even though their perspective may appear to be from the opposite side. By listening to each other's story, everyone begins to connect in ways they never imagined.

They then discuss the state of civility in the legislature and what they want it to be. The group discusses the barriers to getting there, and finally, they develop a set of actions to remove those barriers. That becomes the plan.

In their years of experience holding workshops in 16 states thus far, NCID has found legislators raise strikingly similar concerns: We don't socialize together. We are kept away from each other. We don't have an opportunity to learn about each other. We don't spend any time getting to know each other. Our seating is split to keep us apart.

It's clear that spending more time together and getting to know each other is key to working together. NCID is a leading actor in growing civility, bipartisanship, and ultimately, real solutions to benefit our nation, one state legislature at a time.

———————— ❝ ————————

Joe Scarborough: We've gone all around the country talking with people. Whether it's a liberal or conservative audience, they always ask "Why can't they talk to each other? Why can't they get along?"

Hillary Clinton: There are people on both sides of the aisle. How do we begin to connect with each other? I thought what Patty Murray and Paul Ryan did after the government shutdown in the fall of 2013 was a textbook example. [As budget committee chairs from different political parties in the Senate and House] they were charged with producing a federal budget. They didn't start by walking into a conference room, flanked by their acolytes carrying binders. They had breakfast together. They called each other on the phone. They actually got to know each other as people. What a novel idea! And we've got to get back to that.[123]

Exchange on Morning Joe

---

[123] *Morning Joe,* MSNBC, February 26, 2016

Improving a College's Engagement Between Students and Professors Significantly Improves Students' Retention and Success

————————— **"** —————————

We build long-term support from the bottom up. Top-down support may work for one meeting where the leader makes some pronouncement, but if you truly want to build support that will last it has to come from people committed to the process. It takes more time at first, but it actually saves time in the long run. [124]

Clarence Anthony, Executive Director,
National League of Cities

If you're a college administrator, you want students to complete their degrees because their tuition pays the bills of the school. If you're a professor, you want students to learn, and having them complete their majors produces more graduates that positively contribute to society and perhaps back to the school as alumni. If you're a student, you want your investment in your education—and yourself—to be effective and lead to a better job and hopefully, a better life.

Oakton Community College (OCC), just north of

---

[124] Interview with Clarence Anthony, Executive Director, National League of Cities, December 2015

Chicago, has landed on a strategy that works for all three. They found by training professors to engage with students through a series of structured meetings, that their "persistence," that is, students sticking with their studies and continuing their attendance in the college, increased from 62% to 83% in one year. That's an improvement of more than one-third of students continuing with their studies, achieving success, and far surpassing everyone's goals.[125] They call it the Persistence Project.

To be clear, the Persistence Project requires a significant investment in time and coordination by professors and students, with many meetings. It involves establishing a proactive, basic relationship with every student in the teacher's class. Proactive, because it's not a traditional teacher's "open door" policy, or simply scheduling "office hours" and waiting optimistically for students to show up and discuss their concerns. Rather, it requires reaching out to every single student multiple times during the semester. Here's how it works.

In the first three weeks of class, instructors:

- Commit to learning the names of students.
- Schedule a minimum 15-minute in-person, one-to-one conference with each student. The college recommends even offering the student some form of "credit" as an incentive for attending the meeting. (At the end of this case study, there's a summary of the structure of the one-to-one conference.)
- Set standards, but also balance them to avoid policies

---

[125] Interview with Oakton Community College Professor Michele S. Reznick, August 2016

that doom students to failure. For example, by learning about students' personal lives—which may include holding jobs, raising children, and dealing with limited time—teachers have wide latitude to allow students to make up work, including arranging test taking to match irregular schedules.

- Engage students early. In one interesting requirement, teachers are asked to make an assignment at the beginning of the semester and provide detailed feedback within the first three weeks. The purpose is to connect with students early, see how they respond, and determine if there might be any concerns with schedules. It has less to do with the academic experience and more with establishing a teacher-student relationship.

In addition to engaging students in the subject matter of their class, instructors are also asked to reach out to students on general college activities, including:

- Welcoming new students—that is, actually welcoming them—and acquainting them with resources and opportunities the school has to offer throughout the semester. Instructors also regularly discuss the benefits of achieving an associate's degree. This constant reminder keeps the goal of achievement in the student's mind.
- When possible, instructors are asked to attend one co-curricular activity event with each student. Such examples include opening nights of art exhibitions, theatrical productions, and STEM presentations.

- Offer assistance to students who are struggling in class. Even if a student is unresponsive to a teacher's outreach, the instructor seeks further help for the student through the college's early alert program. The result of making multiple attempts is to try many options to achieve student success.

- As class winds down in the semester, about two weeks before the final exam, instructors say goodbye to their students, encourage them to stay in touch and visit the following semester. Again, the expectation of continuing on helps students feel they are welcome at the school and improves their desire to continue with their education.

The One-to-One Conference

The purpose of the one-to-one conference is to help the teachers and students get to know each other and begin to develop a strong, working relationship. OCC tells teachers it's not difficult to get students to talk, but they're just waiting for someone to ask. Here's the outline teachers follow:

- What was your first reaction to OCC?
- What are your thoughts about career options? How did you get interested?
- What are your interests and hobbies outside of school?
- Are you working now? Tell me about your job. How many hours a week do you work? What do you enjoy about your job?

The content of the conference is different from interview to interview. If a student has a certain passion about a topic or career, teachers focus on that. Others may be returning to school after years in the workforce and be balancing work, family and children. Students determine the direction of the conversation. Also, it is important to discuss class. Here are suggested questions they discuss:

- Did you have any issues obtaining the books for the class? (Follow up on options or provide assistance if there is any trouble.)
- Do you have any concerns with the course requirements? Is there anything I can do to assist or explain?
- When you think about classes where you have learned the most, what did these classes have in common?

Students often reveal gaps in their knowledge about services at the college, and it's good to keep them informed. It's also fair to allow them to ask you questions. It's best to keep them professional.

Good conferences change the way professors/teachers view students. Students can tell if instructors truly respect them and see them as unique individuals who have something to contribute to the class. After the interview, instructors emphasize that they want to see the student not only if they have difficulties in class, but also if they would like to talk in greater depth about the topics and issues discussed in the first conference or even in class.

Program Results

You're probably wondering whether this academic connecting works, and if so, how effective it is. Good question.

It is very effective.

Success is measured by the persistence rate—that is, the
percentage of students that return from one semester to the
next. In its first semester the program was implemented, the
Persistence Project had impressive results.

There were 9,500 students at OCC, with nearly 2,000
involved in the Persistence Project.

Normal persistence from fall to spring semester was
62%.

When a student was involved in just one class where the
teacher was involved in the project, persistence rose for the
next semester to 78%, a 26% improvement.

When a student was involved—by chance—in two
classes with one-to-one conferences, persistence increased
to 82%, a 32% increase over no classes.

And if a student was involved in three classes where
the Persistence Project was used, persistence rose to 83%, a
34% increase.

Clearly, the greatest leap is participating in the project
with at least one class. Nevertheless, it's possible to increase
persistence even higher with multiple classes, although with
diminishing returns.

There are several valuable impacts to greater persistence.
First, students stay in school and learn, a value that trans-
lates to the opportunity for a better job. Second, the school
benefits financially with greater tuition payments leading to

higher graduation rates. Finally, society benefits, as teachers and students learn techniques to connect with each other, skills they can use in a variety of venues to improve the functioning of many organizations and relationships.

———————————— 66 ————————————

You have to be persistent and keep talking with people. There is no collaboration without communication.[126]

Jackie Flowers, CEO, Tacoma, Washington

---

[126] Interview with Jackie Flowers, CEO, Tacoma, Washington, June 2016

A Football Coach Hugs His Players— and Builds a Strong Team

——————— **"** ———————

Find out what people's "touch points" are.
Not physical touch. Find out what makes
them tick, what motivates them, tell them that
you care, and what they do matters to you.[127]
Mike Hyland, Senior Executive, Maryland

The lesson of this case study is not that you should hug your staff so they will feel valued and perform their jobs better. Rather, the lesson is to *tell* your staff, colleagues, or anyone you work with the important role they play in your organization or on your team. In other words, appreciate them in whatever way is meaningful to them.

Tom Herman is by any definition an unusual football coach. As the leader of the University of Houston Cougars football team, he initiated a ritual of appreciation and light affection—hugging—which helped lead the Cougars to a top 10 ranking in 2016. More on that accomplishment in a bit. Herman became so successful and popular, that he got an unsolicited proposal to coach one of the premier college football programs in the nation, the Longhorns of the University of Texas at Austin, which is where he is today.

Of course, you may be wondering how this might apply to you. It started when Coach Herman planted a kiss on the

---
[127] Interview with Mike Hyland, Senior Executive, Maryland, October 2015

cheek of his burly strength coach Yancy McKnight, expressing his appreciation in front of them.[128] After that, Coach Herman extended a similar ritual to every player before every game.

When Herman's team walks into a locker room, they go single file. Herman hugs each player and adds a statement of appreciation, such as "I love this guy." He tells them about their important role on the team. Basically, the coach tells his players how much he appreciates them, and asks them to try their best.

Herman makes the case simply. "How do you motivate a human being? There's two ways: love and fear. And to me, love wins every time."[129]

"He's disrupting a stereotype about boys and men, a notion of masculinity that says boys and men are only driven by the desire for competition and autonomy," said Noibe Way, a psychology professor at New York University. Research shows that humans are not driven by competition and autonomy. Rather, we're driven by the desire to be in connected communities.[130]

Herman prepares his players for this kind of treatment—positive interaction—while recruiting. He tells the parents of high school prospects that he loves and appreciates his players, and treats each of them like his own son.

The takeaway here is not that we should be hugging our staffs or colleagues so they will like us more. Rather, this story of Coach Herman instructs that we need to show

---

[128] *Houston's Coach Pecks Away at Football's Macho Culture, a Kiss at a Time,* Marc Tracy, New York Times, October 15, 2016
[129] Ibid
[130] Ibid

appreciation for those around us. Such gratitude builds a strong bond, which leads to employee loyalty and hard work.

———————————— 66 ————————————

It's important for people to agree on a common goal, the thing they all want to go for. This motivates everyone to make their organization or community a better place. With a common goal, they will sacrifice, and give more of their time and energy.[131]

Jeff Haas, Association Executive, Maryland

—————————————————————————

[131] Interview with Jeff Haas, Association Executive, Maryland, October 2015

Changing People's Minds

———————————— **"** ————————————

If you want the collaboration to work, you have to care what the other party wants. Know and care, or it's not going to be a healthy, win-win collaboration.[132]

John Graham, President and CEO, American Society of Association Executives

This is my favorite chapter, mostly because the issues are difficult and polarizing, and we will see how people from different ends of the belief spectrum came together on a variety of tough topics to achieve understanding. My career has been in the world of public policy and advocacy for three decades, working with new ideas, examining what works, conveying those ideas to sometimes reluctant legislators and stakeholders, and seeking to change and improve the societal landscape. For years, it has fascinated me to examine methods of influence that provide new information and help people change their own minds. I've found there's no magic answer. Everyone is different, and usually a constellation of approaches is needed to bring people to your side. Reading the case studies in this chapter, you should get the feeling that connecting with others and sharing good ideas is within your reach and abilities.

---

[132] Interview with John Graham, President and CEO, American Society of Association Executives, October 2015

————————— **"** —————————

When you put yourself in another person's shoes and try to understand their situation, then you can tailor the collaboration to achieve a good outcome that meets everyone's needs.[133]

Glenn Cannon, former CEO, South Carolina

Reducing Transgender Discrimination

A lot has been written about this first case study. Lengthy articles have appeared in the *New York Times*,[134] NPR's *This American Life*,[135] and *Science Magazine*;[136] probably thousands of words. I'm going to summarize this method of persuasion for you in one word: Emotion.

When you have a really, really tough issue to convince someone to come to your side, facts do not always win the argument. Gun control, abortion, health care, marijuana, and same-sex marriage are just a few polarizing issues many people feel deeply about and have strong opinions that make up their core values. So how do you cut through their entrenched belief system? Connect with them through a similar, shared experience, tell a true story about someone you know, and connect emotionally.

—————————

[133] Interview with Glenn Cannon, former CEO, South Carolina, October 2015
[134] *How Do You Change Voters' Minds? Have a Conversation,* Benoit Denizet-Lewis, The New York Times, April 7, 2016
[135] *The Incredible Rarity of Changing Your Mind,* Ira Glass, This American Life, Episode 555, April 24, 2015
[136] *Durably Reducing Transphobia: A Field Experiment on Door-to-Door Canvassing,* David Broockman and Joshua Kalla, Science Magazine, April 8, 2016, Vol 352, Issue 6282, pp. 220-224

There is a body of research about the impact of advocacy and what it takes to change people's minds. Until recently, much was uncertain. But a series of real-life situations combined with on-the-ground researchers engaged in the projects helped to understand what works.

David Fleisher is the director of Leadership Lab, a progressive advocacy group housed at the Los Angeles L.G.B.T. Center. They had the assignment to canvass voters and seek to change their minds on a highly polarizing issue: transgender prejudice. While there is little research on changing people's minds on this issue, it is true that transgender people face widespread prejudice and discrimination. Fleisher and his team wanted to see if they could change minds and get people to understand the need to reduce transgender discrimination and for transgender people to fit into society.

In their door-to-door canvassing, first they tried basic arguments about fairness for all, which failed. They then turned to emotional experiences, where canvassers were encouraged to talk with voters about anyone they knew who was gay or lesbian, and most important, to speak about their own marriage.

This was highly effective. It turns out that marriage is deeply emotional for the married. As voters talked about their own marriage, canvassers raised the question—wouldn't you want your gay friends to have the same experience?

You might think that being gay was a key ingredient to help convince people, but it's not. Interestingly, just knowing gay or transgender people and describing their experience in society is most important, as well as having a quality conversation with good back-and-forth rapport.

Fleisher, in his canvassing, talked about a friend named Jackson, who grew up as a girl but from an early age knew she wanted to be a boy. He made the transition to live as a man in his twenties, married a woman, and he's much happier.

Remember, Fleisher—the guy doing the convincing—is straight.

He talked about how his friend Jackson had been demeaned in public settings like restaurants. This was effective, again, because people go to restaurants and can imagine how something like this could happen. And in this way, an emotional connection was made that scientists who studied the work of Leadership Lab found impacted people for months or longer after the interaction.

The key ingredients turned out to be 1) listening to people, who shared a lot of information about their own lives and had a lot to say, and 2) developing an appropriate story about the need to treat transgender people fairly, which reflected the personal life experience of the individuals to whom they were talking.

Likewise, if you want to convince someone of something, you need to know a bit about their history and beliefs, and work from that experience to find common ground and shape your arguments. Meet them where *they are,* and use *their* experience to help shape the conversation.

———————————— **"** ————————————

If people feel listened to, the chance of bonding is much greater. It's also likely they will believe the collaboration was successful.[137]

Tom Taylor,
Professor Emeritus, Tallahassee, Fla.

---

[137] Interview with Tom Taylor, Professor Emeritus, Tallahassee, Fla., June 2016

The Incredible Value of Story Exchanges

In this case study, high school students from two very different schools in New York—one public in a working-class neighborhood and the other private with high annual tuition—came together to achieve greater understanding and dissolve preconceived notions about each other.[138]

They used a method developed and promoted by the group Narrative 4, which facilitates story exchanges between groups with significant differences to effectively build bridges and tear down barriers that separate.[139]

Ethical Culture Fieldston School is a private high school in the Bronx, New York City, with annual tuition north of $43,000. University Heights, in the South Bronx, is a public school in one of the poorest congressional districts in the United States. Without being specific about describing the students, I think we can assume that they come from different ends of the socio-economic spectrum: predominantly minority and poor-to-middle-class at University Heights, and middle-class-to-wealthy at Fieldston.

The schools agreed to conduct a story exchange, where students from each school paired off and described themselves to each other. Their goal was to tell each other's story later in the day, so listening carefully was key. After a few hours of meeting, all the pairs returned as a group, and each student was responsible for telling their partner's story in the first person. The goal was to break stereotypes through empathy by walking in each other's shoes.

---

[138] *The Tale of Two Schools*, John Lovell, Deputy Editor, The New York Times Magazine, May 2, 2014
[139] Narrative4.com

The mission of Narrative 4 is to "harness the power of the story exchange to equip and embolden young adults to improve their lives, communities, and the world." Basically, this is values education, with an emphasis on personal responsibility, character, cultural understanding, and ethical behavior. They turn empathy into action, by making people aware that the world is a smaller place when we know each other better.

The story exchange is based on the idea that by knowing the story of another person, we are able to understand one another better.

The Yale Center for Emotional Intelligence documented that schools using story exchanges have better academic and classroom climates. Furthermore, students are less likely to feel negative emotions and more likely to feel positive emotions in school. The data show about a 20% improvement in positive emotions, and only a slight reduction in negative emotions. The results show the process of story exchanges works.[140]

The concept of story exchanges may appear forced. Why, you might ask, do I need to use a formulaic process just to talk to another human being? I think I can do this on my own.

The work of Narrative 4 shows it works—that using a formula gets people to engage who might not otherwise take the time to get to know each other. The idea is the same as what I discussed in the Executive Summary and the section on the Master of Connecting. Sharing personal stories

---

[140] Emotion Revolution Survey conducted by the Yale Center for Emotional Intelligence, narrative4.com

allows people who don't know each other well to quickly engage, bond, build trust, and subsequently, work together.

Liberals and Conservatives Come to an Understanding on Climate Change

There are many polarizing "left vs. right" issues in society today, including abortion, health care, and gun control. *Sierra Magazine* reported in 2017 an amazing story of how two groups of people in Minnesota, far apart on the political spectrum, were able to bridge the divide and speak civilly about one of those issues, climate change.[141] They call the process Rural Climate Dialogues.

For the participants to successfully bridge the gap there were three vital elements. The first was the commitment to spend time discussing the topic, and to do so with experts who could address every issue scientifically. The second was small group discussion, where all perspectives were heard and discussed. Finally, there was the opportunity for self-persuasion, whereby individuals had ample time to consider all the facts and discussion together—the science and political activity surrounding climate change—and come to their own conclusion.

Climate change is a global problem, and it is a slow-moving generational issue.[142] It's difficult to see changes on a daily basis, but when we look at trends over the past decades, it's easy to see that something is changing with the global environment. Winter is shorter; hotter places are

---

[141] *Talking About Climate Change in Trump Country,* Madeline Ostrander, Sierra Magazine, December 14, 2017
[142] *What's Driving Our Climate and Energy Divide,* Amy Harder, Axios, August 20, 2018

hotter and drier; bird migration patterns are changing, and we're seeing more intense hurricanes and wildfires, to name a few of the impacts.

While the science leans in the direction that the Earth's climate is changing, many people consider the issue to be partisan. Like abortion, health care and gun control, climate change has moved to a similar category of tribal politics, where liberals and conservatives take sides in the debate. I argue that each group also is to blame, as conservatives tend to question the science and long-term trends, and liberals exaggerate claims that the sky is falling and every catastrophe is linked to global warming. As a result, no one listens to each other. They even laugh at the other tribe's "stupidity."

As a side note, I have worked in the field of climate change and energy since the early 1980s. At that time the concern was, coming out of the colder decade of the 1970s, global cooling. Wha—? Yes, at that time global temperatures were fluctuating and we were on a slight downward trend. There was even talk of a new Ice Age. Since then, however, global temperatures have climbed steadily, and also our ability has improved to measure and monitor temperatures around the world. For many years, I wasn't completely sure what to think about it, balancing the science, my beliefs, and trying to understand the skeptics' concerns. I've now arrived at a "centrist-action" position, so let me simply say this about climate change: the climate is changing. It always has and always will. The question is how much are humans contributing to this change, and is it an irrevocable, upward trend of warming? Whether you agree or disagree with human-influenced climate change, I think it's difficult to argue that all the tons of chemical emissions we pump daily into the atmosphere from power plants and cars have zero influence. So let's agree that the impact to the planet of these emissions is greater than zero. Then we get to the next question, what should we do about it? And the answer, I believe—and this is just me—is let's do everything we can that is economically sensible to reduce the stuff we put into the air. I call that a "No Regrets" policy. In most cases, actions to mitigate climate change make economic as well as environmental sense. The data need to be presented in a straightforward manner with this argument in mind; that is, what is the impact and how much does it cost? Nevertheless, it's difficult for people on either end of the political spectrum to see a common-sense way forward. That's because the debate is generally presented, at one end, as either the science is wrong, or at the other end, we have to take drastic lifestyle-changing measures like stop driving cars. Neither of these is a sensible way forward, and ultimately, the purpose of the Rural Climate Dialogues was to cut through the rhetoric, seek greater understanding, and perhaps find that middle ground.

With this backdrop, the Institute for Agriculture and Trade Policy (IATP) and the Jefferson Center at the University of Minnesota, which facilitates political discussions, organized the series of Rural Climate Dialogues to see if they could bring people together from across the political spectrum with differing views on climate change, discuss the changing climate, and see if they could come to some agreement or consensus.

In the climate dialogue reported on by *Sierra Magazine*,

there were nine women and nine men—five Republicans, five Democrats, eight independents—all with a mix of education and race. It was a balanced socioeconomic group but also had the potential to devolve into a shouting match.

They began with a detailed presentation from a University of Minnesota climatologist, who showed data on the international climate situation as well as discussing local changes people had seen across Minnesota. They talked about changing weather patterns, floods, severe storms that were expanding in frequency, and the region's water issues. This brought the global issue home in a way everyone could relate to.

By the end of the third day of discussions, two important things happened. First, the participants were getting along, and they even drafted a collective statement on climate change with recommendations for action by county officials. Second, many of them were changing their minds about the cause and impact of climate change.

When we hear about a politically charged issue, it's usually in the context of some belief system. They may be topics on Fox News or MSNBC, which many recognize are pseudonyms for the right and left. Rush Limbaugh has said repeatedly that climate change is a left-wing issue. But when we sit down together to calmly walk through the evidence, there's a greater opportunity to contemplate. And this is exactly what happened. Facts were presented. Questions were asked. Statements were challenged. This occurred repeatedly such that everyone on both sides got their questions fully answered. Rather than following the Pied Piper of tribal politics, each person came to their own conclusion. They no longer saw climate change as something tied to their particular sense of self or their tribe, but rather, an issue with its own set of facts to be considered. Self-persuasion kicked in and people developed their own opinions.

In the end, of the 18 original people in this dialogue group, 10 initially said they were sure or extremely sure climate change was real. Afterwards, that number went up to 17.

One unintended consequence was learning that on difficult issues like this, many people 1) don't know where to begin, and 2) rarely have the opportunity to discuss an issue in depth. This raises another important point—there's value in just getting together with people from "the other side." Putting yourself in the same room and trusting that it will all work out is a big part of the process for connecting. Proximity works.

This is probably the big lesson from the Rural Climate Dialogues—understanding begins community by community and conversation by conversation. We have to take that important step and be willing to have an open discussion.

———————— ❝ ————————

The kitchen table is the most important tool you have to reshape your community. Preparing a home-cooked meal and inviting people over, both those we know and those we want to know, forces us to find common ground.[143]
Erick-Woods Erickson, conservative blogger

—————————————————————

[143] *How to Find Common Ground,* Erick-Woods Erickson, The New York Times, September 30, 2017

Connecting as a Community

———————— **"** ————————

We have more means at our disposal to communicate, to find out what's going on, to listen to other points of view, but I think listening is really important, and there's not a lot of that going on anywhere. It's good to have ideas, but it's okay to take a minute and just hear what someone else says before you attack them.[144]

Viggo Mortensen, Jr., Actor

———————————————————

Here are two case studies of organizations working in local communities to help people engage civilly with each other and work to find solutions that benefit their common purpose.

The Village Square

Imagine a world… where people all along the political spectrum get together for a meal and talk about controversial issues impacting their community, state and nation. They talk openly, debate, and achieve greater understanding— not necessarily developing solutions, but at least achieving greater understanding.

No, I am not making this up. It exists in Tallahassee, Florida, and it's called The Village Square.[145]

———————

[144] *Real Time with Bill Mahr,* HBO, Season 14, No. 23, July 15, 2016
[145] I served on the Board of Directors for The Village Square in 2015-16, attended many events since its inception, and spoke and moderated at several meetings.

The Village Square (TVS) is a non-partisan public educational forum on matters of local, state, and national importance.[146] It is dedicated to providing factual accuracy in civic and political debate by promoting civil discourse on divisive issues, and recalling the history and principles at the foundation of our democracy. That's basically their mission statement.

TVS believes in the power of dialogue and disagreement inside American communities, because that's where human connections are built most naturally, and investments in creating social capital can accelerate and scale to a wider, societal level. The organization conducts a variety of programming centered around civility and community-building (especially among political opposites). TVS works with a variety of community partners, offering more than 30 gatherings per year. Events and programs are created with the intent of building community, fostering dialogue, encouraging disagreement, and ultimately, increasing empathy among the participants. Their model is particularly compelling at a time when, as a society, we're avoiding contact with people who don't look or think like we do—the very contact that Haidt and Iyer's work suggests we need to have more.

To get a flavor of what The Village Square is, it's best to just look at what it does. It convenes meetings at local venues in Tallahassee, hires a restaurant to cater, picks a topic that is important to Tallahasseans locally or a state or national topic, brings in two to four speakers from myriad sides of the issue, and lets them duke it out, civilly. There is rarely a winner in these discussions, but there always is

---

[146] tlh.villagesquare.us

greater understanding on both sides. The audience consists of random locals from all parts of the political spectrum, and the discussion is spirited.

Programs are wide ranging and designed to be socially interesting enough to get citizens away from their electronics and back to connecting, face-to-face, in the "public square." They include activities, like getting to know your city and county commissioners better (through speed dating), and discussions, including regional issues such as should the community build a new power plant, to broad philosophical issues, like what would the Founding Fathers think of government and the state of civic dialogue today. TVS is not afraid to address tough topics and have also tackled thorny issues like gun control, healthcare, climate change, entitlement spending, and tribal politics. They embrace the notion that difference of opinion is a generative force in a healthy democracy that helps us address the big problems with broad and creative thinking.

The website's blog is a fantastic resource of information about public dialogue, and how best to achieve it.[147] TVS's principal is Liz Joyner, an energetic, devoted, creative, action-filled civic-minded person who lives the ethic of creating a more perfect union.

The Village Square started, effectively, in 2006 when the city of Tallahassee and a group of publicly owned electric utilities in Florida sought to build a new coal power plant. There was a big public debate in Tallahassee, and a voter referendum about whether the community should invest in the plant.

---

[147] tlh.villagesquare.us/blog

Key local leaders took opposite sides in the debate. Allan Katz, a Democratic City Commissioner, was strongly opposed to the coal plant. Bill Law, a Republican and President of Tallahassee Community College, was a proponent. They were also friends, who worked together on a variety of issues, but on this particular topic they were diametrically opposed.

The debate in the community was spirited, though it lacked constructive engagement and sometimes got nasty. On the contrary, the private discussions between Allan and Bill were honest, smart, civil, and even humorous at times. Liz Joyner worked with Allan as his campaign manager, and became aware of their meetings. Liz began thinking... could this type of conversation, this engaging political discourse on a different issue, be expanded community-wide?

Hence, The Village Square was born.

The organization is funded in a variety of ways, and like many non-profits, it's sometimes "hand-to-mouth." There are member dues, sponsorships, grants, and special projects from local governments, to name a few. The board of directors consists of many community leaders who help connect to contributions as well, but basically, funding is a continuous challenge. It's an upbeat challenge, as The Village Square is a labor of love many people in the community care deeply about because of their constructive mission to promote civil discourse and make individuals better at tackling important issues.

TVS offers consultation and programmatic support to other community-based groups that are interested in gathering their community across differences of color, creed, and political ideology. In a project called Respect + Rebellion (respectandrebellion.com), they also offer campus and community groups across the country a unique twist on a speakers' bureau. They have assembled pairs of speakers who disagree on divisive issues but have enduring respectful relationships despite their disagreements. These pairs are role models for the very connectedness this book is about.

I personally cannot say enough positive things about The Village Square. Check it out for yourself. If you're interested in civil community dialogue on polarizing issues, this is one of the most successful organizations bringing it all together.

—————————— **"** ——————————

We had a great group of people, who worked extremely hard, but weren't working as a true team. Then we got them in a room and had lunch together. They ate, talked and built relationships. That lead to an innovative collaboration of new ideas and programs.[148]
Ursula Schryver, Association Executive, Virginia

Better Angels

Better Angels is a relatively new organization, formed in 2016. By their own account, "Better Angels is a bipartisan citizen's movement to unify our divided nation. By bringing red and blue Americans together into a working alliance, we're building new ways to talk to one another, participate together in public life, and influence the direction of the nation."[149]

[148] Interview with Ursula Schryver, Association Executive, Virginia, October 2015
[149] better-angels.org

The goal of Better Angels is to reduce political polarization by bringing liberals and conservatives together to understand each other beyond the stereotypes by which everyone typically defines these two groups. They seek to form community alliances composed of both "red" and "blue" people; they teach skills for communicating across political differences, and they seek to depolarize society, or at least argue against it. They don't want people trying to convince each other, but rather, to better understand each other. Better Angels does not to seek to change people to take on a different opinion, but instead, to seek understanding that there are a variety of perspectives and opinion-holders.

Better Angels began when founder David Blankenhorn began talking with people in Mississippi after the extremely polarizing 2016 presidential election. He and Lead Organizer David Lapp wanted to give people a way to bridge their differences, not so much to convince each other, but rather, just to talk civilly and with respect.

Blankenhorn has been known to say "It's not necessarily about compromise, or a muddle to the middle. Rather, let's get back to factual disagreements."[150]

Two of their workshops are described on their website. The "Red/Blue Workshop" brings together seven conservative-leaning participants and seven progressive-leaning participants for three hours of moderated activities and discussions that clarify disagreements, reduce stereotyped

---

[150] Steve Spher, Co-Chair, Better Angels Sacramento Alliance, at Better Angels Forum on the Media's Role in Polarizing America, Trinity Cathedral, Sacramento, Calif., October 27, 2018

thinking, and begin building the relationships needed to find common ground. (The same workshop can also be delivered in a full-day, seven-hour session.) Their "Skills Workshop" teaches practical approaches for having better conversations with friends and family members with whom it's possible to sometimes have strong political disagreements.

The organization is funded with member dues (minimum of $10), and grants. Currently there are 4,000 dues-paying members, and Better Angels aspires to 10,000. There are 12,000 subscribers on their distribution list, which continues growing. They have a national presence, with members in every state. Funding is also augmented with foundation grants.

The future is promising. There is significant interest from the news media, and the organization was featured on ABC's Nightline. They held a national convention, with half "red and blue" attendance. In the future, Better Angels hopes to reach out to elected officials and encourage that transition of civility in state legislatures and Congress.

One of the key elements of the organization is to help people find common ground, to see another individual first as a person, not an enemy. They focus on the human level first, then on issues. The organization does not emphasize changing minds, but rather, to get to know each other, share opinions, and achieve a level of respect. This is consistent with the thesis of this book: to share personal stories. It's a foundational element.

Here are Better Angels' principles:[151]

---

[151] better-angels.org

For citizens

- Try to understand the other side's point of view, even if we don't agree with it.
- Engage those we disagree with, looking for common ground and ways to work together.
- Support political ideas and leaders that bring us together rather than divide us.

For civic groups and faith communities

- When feasible and to the degree consistent with your mission, seek opportunities to work for depolarization.
- In any activity aimed at depolarization, seek to ensure that liberals and conservatives in roughly equal numbers conceive, design, fund, organize, lead, and evaluate the activity.

For scholars

- When feasible and to the degree consistent with your vocation, seek opportunities to study depolarization and make recommendations for the future.
- In any collaborative intellectual work on polarization, seek to ensure that liberals and conservatives in roughly equal numbers conceive, design, fund, organize, lead, and evaluate the work.

For media

- Know and respect the difference between reporting and editorializing.

- Know and respect the difference between news and entertainment.
- On TV, radio, podcast, and other programs, don't have guests who only repeat talking points for their side.
- On TV, radio, podcast, and other programs, invite guests with opposing views who'll talk *with* rather than *at* or *about* each other.
- On shows you host and in commentaries you offer, engage your opponents' best arguments, not their worst or most extreme.
- In conversations you lead involving disagreements, push for accurate rather than exaggerated, imagined, or feigned disagreement.
- In reporting or commenting on news, favor substance over superficiality.
- When you inadvertently say or write something factually incorrect, publicly correct it.
- When a guest on your program says something factually incorrect, give them an opportunity publicly to correct it.

For politicians

- Treat opponents with respect.
- Seek opportunities to acknowledge shared values with opponents.
- Seek opportunities to find political common ground with opponents.
- Engage your opponents' best arguments.

- Decline to engage in personal attacks.
- Do not presume that your opponents are acting in bad faith.
- When taking a stance on an issue, show voters your rationale and evidence, cite your sources, and present your argument in a way that permits fact-checking.
- Advocate for principles of depolarization as one of your main priorities.

The organization also brings together scholars, writers and citizens from across the political spectrum to engage in what they call "the Better Angels Way." That is, constructively engaging with opposing points of view rather than name-calling and partisan posturing. The organization also has an active media presence, writing blogs and publishing podcasts with participants from different ends of the political spectrum talking to each other about various issues, such as capitalism vs. welfare, and video stories on their approach. They have a robust website with great information about polarization and how to minimize it.

One of their articles bears repeating here, Ten Better Angels Skills:[152]

Five Basic Skills

1. Listen to understand rather than to prepare your rebuttal. If you couldn't accurately summarize what the other person just said, you haven't listened.
2. Be curious ("Why do you see it this way?") rather

---

[152] better-angels.org

than argumentative ("How could you possibly see it this way?")

3. Make sure you understand the other's view before you disagree with it. ("Let me see if I understand what you are saying...")

4. Use I-statements ("This is how I see it") more often than truth-statements ("This is how it is.") If you are citing facts, give your source rather than just saying it's true.

5. Avoid characterizing the other side's position in your own terms rather than theirs. ("Your side sees immigration as a threat to the country." "Your side is for open borders.")

Five Advanced Skills

1. Start with an underlying value or perspective you may agree on before saying what you disagree with. ("Sounds like we both want an immigration system that is fair to immigrants and good for the country.")

2. Offer something critical of your own side ("My party's leaders have let money interests influence them too much.")

3. Offer something positive about the other side ("Your party has picked up on the concerns of people that my party has ignored.")

4. When disagreeing, keep acknowledging the other's view ("I hear your concern about this policy backfiring. My own view is..."

5. If the other person escalates, don't go there ("I get

your point and I know we differ a lot on this. Shall we let it go or keep talking?")

Membership in Better Angels is open to all for just $10. Members have the opportunity to organize workshops, build alliances, and be trained as moderators.[153]

───────────── " ─────────────

I really do believe the middle is where we get things done. If you aren't willing to compromise, we never accomplish things for [our] families.[154]

Former U.S. Senator
Claire McCaskill, D-Missouri

───────────────────────────────

[153] better-angels.org
[154] *The Battle for Missouri,* Part One, The Daily Podcast, The New York Times, October 16, 2018

Giving the Gift of Connection

A personal story…

Years ago, I went to the supermarket to buy groceries. I went through the checkout line like I'd done countless times before, except this time was slightly different. My 10-year-old daughter, Emily, was with me.

I finished the transaction and Emily and I began pushing the shopping cart toward our car. We hadn't taken five steps from the checkout counter when Emily turned to me and said, "Dad, you weren't very nice to that woman."

I frowned and thought carefully about the interaction.

"I wasn't not nice," I replied defensively. "I was, ummm, neutral."

What actually happened was the young lady at the checkout register tried to engage me in friendly conversation, asking a series of pleasantries. I answered every one of her questions—each with one word.

"Did you find everything okay?"

"Yep."

"Sure is hot out there."

"Yep."

"How about those Noles!" (Our local college football team.)

"Yep."

Emily continued, "Well I don't know how you see it, but from my perspective, you weren't very nice."

We walked in silence to our car. I put the groceries in the back, got in, started the ignition, and turned to Emily.

"You're right," I said. "I can see how my short, one-word answers could be perceived as being not very nice. I'll try to do better."

I really gave it thought. Is it in me to reach out and be nice to strangers I don't really feel like talking to? My wife June, who easily talks with strangers, was a great role model. Rather than staying silent during these impromptu interactions, maybe I could join in, or even initiate a conversation.

I decided that engaging in conversation with new people was a gift from me. I would do everything I could to give them the gift of friendliness, the gift of a pleasant moment.

From that moment on, I've made it a life mission to brighten the lives of strangers whenever I get the chance. It's not easy, because I'm sometimes restrained and must remind myself to make the effort to be outgoing. When I take the initiative, it's noticeable, as it almost always puts a smile on someone's face. I feel better too, and while I'm not seeking to get anything out of it, I believe I've gotten better service as a result. It's a two-way gift of kindness and happiness. This may sound corny, but unless you've experienced it, you'd be amazed how nice the exchanges are. Most of all, I walk away happier, having brightened someone else's day.

Try it yourself.

Eleven Lessons from the Case Studies

- Get closer to people with different perspectives. Seek to understand them and accept the diverse quilt of society. Without such understanding and appreciation, it's easier to fall prey to common misperceptions about other races and cultures.

- Everyone has the capacity to connect, even burly men who may not have a lot of experience expressing themselves. Once people learn techniques to connect, however, their capacity to communicate and connect with each other is profound.

- Working together as a well-functioning team can take place with nearly any group of people from various backgrounds, ages, and races. The most important element is that teammates devote time learning about each other, taking care that everyone has about the same amount of time sharing, and in the process, becoming interested in each other. Telling a group about equity of voice—the goal of sharing equally—can get people in the right state of mind. A guide in the group, who seeks that everyone share somewhat equally, can help this process along.

- One of the most polarizing institutions in the United

States—Congress—is capable of bipartisanship. A handful of elected officials has proved it. Their secret: sitting down with each other over dinner and learning about each other's backgrounds, important events that shaped their lives and outlooks, and what inspired them serve the public.

- While connecting often happens organically—that is, on its own—it can also be facilitated. Establishing a meeting structure, with suggested questions, can speed the process along.

- Telling colleagues about the importance of their role on the team can have a profound impact on motivating individuals to perform better together and for each other.

- Getting people to talk about something they have in common, like a shared experience (their opinions on marriage, for example), talking about how they grew up, or having them talk about a controversial issue has the effect of allowing people the experience of "being heard." It is a strong technique that allows all parties in a conversation to feel that their opinion matters, and has the effect of opening minds to new information.

- Entire communities, with people from various political perspectives, can follow a process to engage, learn, and achieve deeper understanding to help address and advance local issues. People have to engage enough to first learn about each other, and then they can begin to address and resolve tough community issues.

- When meeting new people, learning about where they are from, what they like spending time doing, where they might be going on vacation next, or just simply what has gotten their attention in the past week, are good open-ended questions that inspire deeper conversation and the opportunity to significantly learn more about each other in a short amount of time.

- Take the initiative to make your interactions positive. Be the first to be friendly, and give others the gift of a pleasant moment that will brighten their day.

And One More: What to Say When Someone is Hurting

- Sadly, at some point our relatives, friends and colleagues will experience divorce, family trauma, sickness, and death. When someone we know is distracted, hurting or grieving, it's not appropriate to say "Mornin' Dave! How are you doing?," or some other chirpy greeting. We should not ignore them either, because feeling supported and cared for is an important form of connection. People who are hurting emotionally, often are just trying to get through the day. When you know someone is experiencing difficulties in their personal life, you can say something like: "How's today, Jeremy?" or "Hey Wendy, it's good to see you." Expressions like these help your colleague, friend or relative know you are aware of their situation, and most important, that you care about them. Don't expect much in response, but persist in your outreach and concern. Reaching out, however simple, lets them know you care, and your bond will strengthen.

PART 5.
AND IN CONCLUSION...

Now it's your turn. You have the tools and have seen how others have done it themselves. In many settings, choosing to connect made the situation better and helped various individuals and groups work better together and accomplish an important goal. There are four elements to remember about the secret to powerful connections and getting along with others in business and life:

1. <u>Share Personal Stories</u>: Get closer to and learn about others, where they're from, some life experiences and interests, and also share the same about yourself.
2. <u>Talk Equally</u>: Be conscious of the amount of time everyone speaks, and guide interactions so individuals share about the same amount of time. Officially, it's called "Equity of Voice." The amount of time each person speaks doesn't have to be precise or forced, and it works best when it occurs naturally or is steered lightly.

3. <u>Assume Positive Intent</u>: People generally want their colleagues and peers to succeed, and are not out to get you. Since you can control only your behavior, interact with the expectation that everyone is positive and striving for a win-win outcome.
4. <u>Persist</u>: It takes time, and it works. For many, it works right away. For others, it may take longer. Keep trying. It may not work overnight, but in almost all cases, it does work eventually.

And now I'm eager to learn from you. Please share with me your stories of connection. How did it go? What were the circumstances before, and then after you connected? What hurdles did you have to overcome? What techniques worked for you? What was the outcome?

Please... tell me more.

CONTACT INFORMATION

For more information, and to contact Barry about speaking engagements:

Email: **barry@barrymoline.com**

Website: **barrymoline.com**

Barry welcomes you to connect with him for conversation and consultation. You can learn more about leadership, motivation, communication, persuasion, and happiness at Barry's website. There you can sign up for his newsletter and engage with Barry on social media. His goal is to help you and your organization achieve the highest level of success.

ACKNOWLEDGMENTS

———————— " ————————

If you see a turtle on a fence post, he probably had help getting there.[155]
Little Jimmy Dickens, Country Singer

This book was written with the support of many people, a lot of research, many fortuitous moments, and a heavy dose of loving support.

A book about working together probably should be written by actually working together with someone. This book started as a co-authored project with my friend Mark Schumann. We were working on a project in a small Florida town, Vero Beach, where city leaders were debating some controversial decisions about the future of their community. The infighting was heated, and often ugly. People didn't just disagree, they went out of their way to first insult each other, then disagree. At one point Mark and I asked each

---

[155] Pinterest.com, and Wikipedia: *Little Jimmy Dickens*

other, "Does anyone get along anywhere?" We started investigating, and found many communities, businesses, schools, non-profits, and teams who were not only effective at cooperating, but also achieving amazing results. Encouraged, we brainstormed together for several days in Santa Fe and outlined the book, originally titled "C Factors," for communicating, collaborating and connecting. A few months into the project, Mark—also an outstanding professional photographer—found a different calling. He wanted to focus attention on the growing problem, and potential solutions, for homelessness. He sadly told me he needed to step away from our collaboration and follow this passion. Fortunately, Mark has finished his project, a beautiful book of portraits and stories dedicated to resolving homelessness in America. Check it out at homelessinalandofplenty.com. Mark is a warm-hearted soul, extremely curious and compassionate about others, and I am honored to call him a friend.

I talked with well over a hundred people in researching, writing, and publishing this book. Everyone was helpful, whether it was sitting for an interview, connecting me with someone they knew, or sending me information to review. In one instance, I was having trouble making contact with the people from Better Angels in New York. On a random Saturday evening, my wife and I went to dinner for the first time at the home of new friends, Eric and Eileen, and surprisingly, they had a Better Angels sign in their front yard. It turns out—serendipitously—that Eric is a local coordinator for Better Angels in Sacramento, where we live. Within days he helped connect me with their headquarters to arrange an interview, the last one I needed to complete this book. There were many other supportive moments, and for all the people who helped in so many ways, I am grateful for their time and expertise.

There was also a lot of encouragement. When you're writing a book, there's no task master other than yourself. Giving up at any time is an easy option. Luckily, I have many people in my life who frequently encouraged me and gave me the confidence to continue. My mom told me how proud she was of the effort. My sisters Michele and Bonnie remained impressed and helped wherever they could. And my friends kept up the motivational talks to keep me going through those times when I was tired or wasn't making the time to write.

Daughters Emily and Lily had special roles. After finishing much of the research, I was having trouble sitting down to write. At the same time, Emily was working on her PhD dissertation in linguistics, and was also having a tough time writing. We committed to supporting each other by meeting weekly for several hours at a local coffee shop, Old Soul. For about the first hour we'd shop online for things neither of us needed. Then we finally got down to business and made progress, one paragraph at a time. After months of meeting and writing, we both had enough momentum where we could each see the finish line. I know this book would never have been finished without the two of us spending all that time together, and I so appreciate Emily for helping to make that happen.

In a bizarre and humorous turn of events, one conclusion of Emily's PhD dissertation found that tutors who spend time learning about their students' personal lives, and also share information about themselves, have more effective learning outcomes teaching English as a second language to adults.[156] That is, sharing personal stories works to enhance relationships and improve learning. What's amusing is that we sat there for months, side by side in that coffee shop working on unrelated projects, both finding similar results.

Lily had multiple roles. She shared her leadership and connection experience as president of her University of Florida Intercollegiate Ultimate Frisbee team, as well as enthusiastically encouraging me to keep going during the dark days of writer's block. Lily always impresses me with her strong ethics and morals, inspiring simplicity, as well as her desire to leave everything better off than how she found it, especially the Earth. I'm proud that both Emily and Lily are incredible connectors, bringing people together around them in various ways to accomplish amazing goals in whatever they touch.

Finally, my wife June, my closest connector. Aside from being my life partner, lover, confidante, and moral compass, she keeps our lives grounded so it's easy for me to take the time to do the many projects and activities I continuously seem to take up. As a book author herself, she blazed the path for me, setting the example of how it's done, showing me the commitment needed and how to put forth the effort. She is my rock, and more than anyone, this book is dedicated to her.

[156] *L1 and L2 Adult Emergent Literacy: Reading Patterns, Oracy, and Interaction Within an English Literacy Program*, Emily Ariel Moline, PhD Dissertation, University of California, Davis, 2018

CPSIA information can be obtained
at www.ICGtesting.com
Printed in the USA
FSHW011247240819